The Spanish Virgin Islands

by BRUCE VAN SANT

Cruising, diving, snorkeling and fishing

throughout

the Spanish Virgin Islands

IMPORTANT NOTICE:

The chartlets in this guide are intended to assist the reader in following the sailing tactics described, not for taking meaningful measurements for navigation. The prudent mariner will avail himself of official charts and publications, as well as any navigational methods and tools required to ensure the safety of the vessel and the accuracy of navigation. There are no warranties, either expressed or implied, as to the usability of the information contained herein for any purpose whatever.

Distributed by
Cruising Guide Publications
1130-B Pinehurst Road, Dunedin, FL 34698
Phone: (813) 733-5322 • (800) 330-9542 • Fax: (813) 734-8179
Email: cgp@earthlink.net

Art Direction
TOM HENSCHEL

ISBN: 944428-40-1
Printed in the U.S.A.

The Spanish Virgin Islands

Puerto Rico

If you're chartering, why

The Virgin Islands are a lot bigger than other charter companies have been telling you. That's because they don't want you to know.

Sure, there are peaceful, protected waters, lovely beaches and terrific sailing in the 32-mile strip those companies let you explore. (That's an area about half the size of San Francisco Bay or a third of Long Island Sound.) But there is so much more.

Sun Yacht Charters wants you to see <u>all</u> the best Virgin Islands. With us, you're free to sail the entire chain from the Spanish Virgins to the BVI, including unspoiled and uncrowded places you could never visit before, like Culebra and Vieques.

We give you more options, too. Depart from our base at Hodges Creek on Tortola or from our newest base in Marina Puerto del Rey (look for us aboard *La Esperanza*) at Fajardo, Puerto Rico. You can even start your Virgin Islands charter at one Sun Yacht Charters' base and end at the other.

Sun Yacht Charters with Stardust Marine: Spanish Virgin Islands British Virgin Islands St. Martin Antigua Guadeloupe

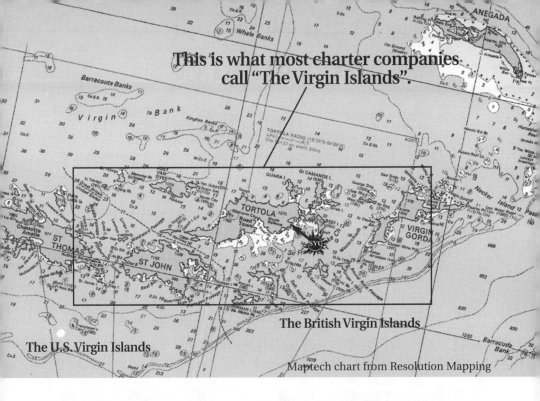

This is what most charter companies call "The Virgin Islands".

The U.S. Virgin Islands

The British Virgin Islands

Maptech chart from Resolution Mapping

not sail all of the Virgins?

At both bases and throughout *our* Virgin Island waters, you'll enjoy Sun Yacht Charters' outstanding personal service, our on-water support, plus the widest choice of monohulls and catamarans, bareboat or crewed. And all this is backed by our unmatched Double Guarantee that ensures our performance and your satisfaction.

So, don't get boxed in on your next charter. Come sail with Sun Yacht Charters. Because, when you come to the Virgin Islands, bigger is better.

Sun Yacht Charters
We guarantee the time of your life.
800-772-3500
59 Union Street, Box 737, Camden, Maine 04843
Fax: 207-236-3972 E-mail: sunyacht@midcoast.com
For crewed yacht inquiries, call toll-free 888-772-3702

Martinique Grenadines French Riviera Corsica Majorca Greece Turkey Tahiti New Caledonia Australia New Zealand

Contents

"La Isla del Encanto" is the name given to Puerto Rico around the world because of the caring people, history and prosperity.

INTRODUCTION

Belonging to the Commonwealth of Puerto Rico, these islands lie between the U.S. Virgin Islands and Puerto Rico, both of which are territories of the United States. They were discovered by Columbus on his second voyage to the New World in 1493.

Columbus named the main island, called Borinquen by the Tainos that lived there, San Juan Bautista to honor Prince Juan, the son of Ferdinand and Isabela. Ponce de LeÛn, who explored the southeast United States, founded Puerto Rico's first settlement and was its first governor.

Many of the smaller islands were alternately ignored or disputed by the European powers during the four centuries in which the main island of Puerto Rico was a colony of Spain. They were ceded by Spain to the United States with the Treaty of Paris in 1898. Puerto Ricans are U.S. Citizens and half are bilingual.

The population is the most affluent in Latin America, but in 1995, 62 per cent of the population was on welfare. Expect to be boarded by the U.S. Coast Guard. In 1995, 25 per cent of the illegal drugs entering the U.S. did so through Puerto Rico.

The Spanish Virgin Islands embrace approximately 400 square sea miles to the west of the U.S. Virgin Islands. Unlike the U.S. Virgin Islands, Puerto Rico has an extensively developed industrial and agricultural infrastructure.

The Spanish Virgins, like the USVI, are entirely dependent on tourism, yet they are many years behind in the development of tourism infrastructure. This is bad for the typical resort tourist, but great for the getaway cruiser and diving enthusiast.

It means unaffected townspeople, undisturbed anchorages, pristine beaches and productive fishing (with a year-round lobster season).

Ashore, the Spanish Virgins offer immersion in the Spanish Caribbean with the escape clause of bilingualism and the convenience of U.S. institutions.

There are four cruising areas in the Spanish Virgins:
• Puerto Rico's East Coast
• La Cordillera
• Culebra
• Vieques

Be sure to schedule ample time to enjoy each of these very special areas.

PUERTO RICO FACTS

Average coastal daytime temperature 73-85 degrees, in the mountains, 5 - 10 degrees cooler; annual rainfall 62 inches.

HISTORY

Puerto Rico was discovered by Columbus in 1493 when the Taino Indians lived on the island. Its present capital, San Juan, was established in 1521. Puerto Rico is now a Commonwealth of the United States. The island's culture is a blend of Indian, African and Spanish and American.

LANGUAGE

Spanish and English are the official languages.

POPULATION

3.5 million with one third of the population concentrated in the San Juan-Bayamon-Carolina metropolitan area.

MONEY & BUSINESS

BANKING HOURS:
Monday to Friday 0830 - 1430.

BUSINESS HOURS:
Monday to Friday 0900 - 1700. Shopping: 0900 - 1800 — Except the malls which are from 1000 - 2100 daily.

CURRENCY & CREDIT CARDS:
The U.S. dollar. Credit cards and Traveler's checks are widely accepted for all places, dining, nightclubs, resorts, and shopping. Major Cards such as American Express, Visa, Diner's Club, Discovery, Mastercard, and other Bank Credit Cards are accepted everywhere.

TAXES & SERVICE CHARGES:
Departure tax - None
Hotels & Casinos - 9%
Hotels - 7%
Service charge - 15%
Import Duty - 6.6%

PUERTO RICO PROFILE

GEOGRAPHY

Situated between the Atlantic Ocean and the Caribbean Sea, Puerto Rico is the easternmost of the Greater Antilles. The 110 by 35 nautical mile island has a central mountain range whichreaches an altitude of 4,389 feet at Cerro la Punta. Numerous rivers flow down the mountains to surrounding coastal plains. The island is approximately 1,000 miles southeast of Miami and about 40 miles from the U.S. Virgin Islands.

TIME

EST +1. GMT (UTC)-4.

CLIMATE

Temperature -
High: Summer - 98 degrees.
Winter - 60 degrees.
Low: Summer - 60 degrees.
Aerage Humidity - 55% day - 80% night.

ASHORE IN PUERTO RICO

TOURING BY RENTAL CAR

Like in North America, one must have access to a car in Puerto Rico. If you decide to rent a car to tour the country, get a road atlas and follow the purple lines, the *Ruta Panoramica*, through the mountains and small towns, staying at designated Paradors, usually historic or otherwise noteworthy inns. A good rule to use while driving: stop at every lechón (roasting pig) at the roadside, buy a beer and rip off a piece of the *lechón*. It's delicious, you'll meet many good Puerto Ricans, and in this manner you'll only make about 20 miles a day on weekends and holidays.

TOURING BY *PÚBLICO*

It is still possible to backpack Puerto Rico like you can in the Dominican Republic. There is not, however, the elaborate public transportation system found in the DR. Like North America, nearly everyone has access to a car, and for those that don't, there is still a good *público* system which has been waning as the island affluence waxes.

Carros P'blicos are automobiles that travel specific routes between towns. They wait in ranks around the town square, or at terminal facilities in cities, until enough passengers have signed up to nearly fill the car. If you wish depart earlier or to travel in comfort, you may buy any unfilled seats. For best results, buy the 3 seats next to the driver. While p'blicos always gather and start from the same place, they deliver passengers to wherever, within reason, they wish to go at the destination town.

In Puerto Rico they are large honky old American cars with about the same interior space as Japanese ones used in the DR. The *públicos* in Puerto Rico cost much more than they do in the DR, but they only cram in 5 instead of 6, and like in the DR, you can always buy vacant seats for more comfort. Every small town has público ranks around the town hall square, except Boquerón. Larger towns have elaborate terminal buildings.

Old San Juan

3

FIESTAS PATRONALES

If you do Puerto Rico in the summer, take lots of time and hit every port. Summer in Puerto Rico is the season of the *Fiestas Patronales* [fee-ACE-tahs pah-tro-NAHL-ace]. These are celebrations each town throws for itself (and theoretically its patron saint) as a way to liven up the summer and the business doldrums.

The *Fiestas* are sequenced to permit the traveling entertainers, rides and food concessions to appear at every one. Yet each *Fiesta* has its own atmosphere as the town turns on for a full week. The *Fiestas* in the smaller towns will bring back the Fourth of Julys of 50 years ago for older cruisers from Main Street, U.S.A. The larger towns and county seats, such as Fajardo, often have fiestas which ring the central plaza for 3 and 4 blocks deep. Each port in Puerto Rico is either at or within a *público* ride from at least 3 *Fiestas*. Some of the entertainment provided at these festivals is world class. You may find yourself face to face with Jose Feliciano or Yolandita Monge.

WEATHER

Weather in the tropical tradewinds belt is seasonally predictable, permitting somewhat reliable cruise planning. Wind strength and direction, and possible swell, are factors to consider in setting a ports and diving itinerary, especially when choosing day anchorages. To help you plan your cruise, here are the annual cycles you can expect.

WINTER MONTHS

December through March, distant northern gales often create swell in exposed northern anchorages, and some day anchorages might be untenable. Fortunately, the lovely harbors of the south coast of Vieques and the reef anchorages of Culebra, Icacos and Palominos are unaffected. Cold fronts that make it this far south are often stalled or have dissipated into troughs which persist for several days. While not good for the avid sailor, these conditions make for fluky winds which in turn create diving and snorkeling opportunities across La Cordillera, in Culebra's outlying keys, and on Vieques' north coast.

SUMMER MONTHS

From late July to early September there may be some "bloom" in the water which can restrict visibility for divers. Sailing is great in the cooling summer trades which make these islands cooler and less humid than most of North America at this time of the year. Long hauls to windward are pleasurable, and anchorages are often empty. Like fronts in the winter, summer tropical waves create breaks in the tradewinds, and otherwise exposed diving sites become open to exploration.

THE BETWEEN MONTHS

April to June is usually too late for strong fronts and too early for organized tropical waves. October and November are, conversely, too early and too late; trade winds moderate and days are clear and sunny. Northerly swells are infrequent and there is minimum chop on Vieques Sound. Diving sites and day anchorages have their highest availability during these months.

AM/VHF WEATHER FORECASTS

Local meteorological and marine reports are given hourly after the news on WOSO San Juan, 1030 KHz Am standard broadcast band. WVVI broadcasts a brief "Sailor's Report" on 1000 KHz AM, at 6:30 a.m. Monday through Friday. This includes the short range NOAA coastal report and the next 12 hours of the National Weather Service's Offshore Report. NOAA broadcasts a continuous Weather Channel on VHF from San Juan, but it is of limited use to the cruiser more than three miles east of the Puerto Rico mainland. VI Radio, however, broadcasts a complete summary of the meterorological, coastal and offshore reports, as well as the Tropical Weather Outlook and Tropical Weather Discussion during hurricane season. This is also continuous and on a VHF Weather Channel which is received in eastern Puerto Rico.

While the coastal reports are fine for most islands and anchorages, if you are out on the open Sound in the daytime, or anywhere east or south of Vieques, you must listen to the Offshore Forecast for the Eastern Caribbean on WVVI's Sailor's Report or on VI Radio's VHF Weather Channel; no other report will do.

SPANISH VIRGIN ISLANDS FACTS

AIRLINES

There are direct flights to Puerto Rico from many US cities. Luis Miñoz International Airport in San Juan, the capital, is the hub of the Americas and serves Europe as well. There is an inexpensive air service to Vieques and Culebra (known as "Isla Nena") from Fajardo and San Juan.

- ACES : (787) 724-2020
- Air Calypso : (800) 253-0020
- Air Canada : (800) 776-30
- American Airlines: (800) 981-4757
- British Airways : (800) 247-9297
- BWIA : (800) 538-2942
- Carnival Air : (800) 274-6140
- COPA : (787) 722-6969
- Delta : (800) 221-1212
- KIWI :(800) 721-5000
- LACSA : (800) 225-2272
- Lufthansa : (800) 645-3880
- Mexicana : (787) 791-7100
- Northwest : (800) 225-2525
- TWA : (800) 221-2000
- United : (800) 241-6522
- USAir : (800) 842-5374

GROUND TRANSPORT

Driving is on the right hand side of the road. The road signs are in Spanish, the distance markers are in kilometers & the gas is sold in litres. Temporary license/permit requirements usually depends on the car rental company's policies. Normally a valid driver's license from your home country will do.

Local services - Regularly scheduled city buses and metered taxis operate through metropolitan San Juan. Intra-island buses also run between San Juan, Mayaguez and Ponce. Inter-island flight service is available from San Juan, Ponce and Mayaguez to Vieques and Culebra.

FERRY

Old San Juan to Cataño: every half hour between 6:00 am to 9:00 p.m.
Fajardo - Vieques - Culebra: passenger and car.

TAXI FARES FROM SAN JUAN AIRPORT

Taxi fares are metered. It is not necessary to agree fares before hand but it's best to ensure the rates befor the cabbie starts the meter.

Fajardo-Culebra-Vieques Ferry at Puerto Real

USEFUL TELEPHONE NUMBERS IN THE CRUISING AREA

Puerto Rico has modern, reliable United States style telephone service (area code 787). A local call costs 10 cents.

During 1996 the area code of Puerto Rico was changed from 809 to 787. The country code is 1. Local information is 411; from outside Puerto Rico dial

1-787-555-1212. For directory assistance to others parts of Puerto Rico, dial 0. Person-to-person, collect and calling card calls are easy to place. At the center of thephone book are blue pages in English.

U.S. COAST GUARD
Search & Rescue, San Juan
    722-2943

NOAA WEATHER SERVICE
San Juan Airport   253-4588

CARIBBEAN STRANDING NET
   399-1904

U.S. FCC — SAN JUAN
   753-4567

CUSTOMS
Culebra Airport   742-3531
Fajardo, Puerto Real
   863-0950 / 0102 / 3250
San Juan Airport
   253-4533 / 34 /37 / 38

CHARTERS
Puerto del Rey
  Tropic Keys Yachts 860-6100
  Club Nautico 860-2400

ENGINE / GENERATOR REPAIR
Marine Energy Service
  Puerto del Rey 863-6965
Re-Power Marine Service
  Fajardo 863-9786

SERVICES & REPAIRS
Puerto del Rey
  Captain Ron 381-9146
  El Espanol 863-6965
Isleta
  Island Marine 382-3051

MARINAS WITH HAUL-OUT
Isleta Marina 384-9032
Puerto del Rey 860-1000
Palmas del Mar 850-2065

CHANDLERS
Abel Marine, Fajardo 860-0945
Basic Marine,
  Puerto del Rey 860-5151
Villa Marina
  El Pescador 863-2455
  Skipper Shop 863-2455

SAILMAKERS / CANVAS
Atalantic Canvas & Sails
  Puerto del Rey 860-1433
Isleta Canvas
  Isleta Marina 376-9324
Fajardo Canvas & Sails
  Villa Marina 863-3761

TOWING
Abel Marine
  Fajardo (Ch.16) 860-0945

CRUISING INFORMATION

Barracuda

CUSTOMS AND IMMIGRATION

The sailor travels in and out of the U.S. Virgin Islands and Puerto Rico as one might between New York and New Jersey. You are in the United States of America, with one exception: since the USVIs are considered a duty free port, one must clear in to Puerto Rico upon arriving from the USVI, but not upon arrival to the USVIs from Puerto Rico.

If arriving from either the U.S. or the British Virgin Islands, it will be necessary to clear customs. From Culebra, call 742-3531 or take the five minute walk to the airport. At any of the marinas in Fajardo, call the harbormaster on VHF channel 16.

In Fajardo, during regular working hours, call customs at 863-0950/0102/3250. Outside of regular business hours, call 253-4533/34/37/38 at the San Juan airport. Customs in Fajardo is located at the old customs house on the waterfront by the ferries in Puerto Real (see chartlet). Vessels not sporting a valid customs entry decal shall be asked to pay $25 for a new one. See the section on Culebra for more details.

Non-US vessels, and vessels with nonresident *aliens* aboard (what Americans call foreigners, I'm afraid), must check into Puerto Rico at official ports of entry, which means Culebra or Fajardo on the east coast.

U.S. vessels can clear Customs in Puerto Rico by phone from their landfall.

Customs will advise if they want your boat present when you call them. Customs requires a current sticker (*a cruising permit* for *citizens!*) in both the USVIs and Puerto Rico. They'll tell you where and how to buy one if you don't have one.

8

PUERTO RICO PORTS OF ENTRY

Call US Customs between the hours of 0800 and 1700 at the following:

Coast	City	Location	Phone Numbers
west coast	Mayaguez	commercial pier	831-3342,43
south coast	Ponce	Playa Ponce	841-3130,31
east coast	Fajardo	Puerto Real Customs	863-0950, 4075
north coast	San Juan	Muñoz Marín Airport	253-4533, 34,35,36
Vieques	Isabel	airport	741-8366
Culebra	Dewey	airport	742-3531
St.Thomas, USVI	Charlotte Amalie	ferry dock	
St.Johns, USVI	Cruz Bay	ferry dock	
St.Croix, USVI	Christiansted	dockside	

Outside office hours call the office in San Juan at 253-4533 or 253-4536.

Stingray

TIPS ON CLEARING CUSTOMS EASILY

I am convinced the customs and immigration officials of the world meet every February in Den Hague to formulate plans for confounding guide writers. They get merit points for attending seminars in changing procedures rapidly. Find a good bartender or a cheap gourmet cafe and they'll be around at least six months, long enough to make the final proofs. Then the bartender will run off with the cook the day you go to press. Customs, however, has a plan. They change it every ten boats that enter. If someone tells you, "Here's how you clear customs in Gerfunknik!" you are probably better off doing the opposite of that which is suggested. That said I'll try my best to ease the experiences for you, but you won't get temporal detail.

9

In general, your experience with clearance officials will be dependent on your presentation. Have your boat and yourselves presentable. Have your papers in order: ships papers, passports and clearance out (*despacho* or *zarpe*) from your last port. Crew lists should b prepared with the name, address and passport number of each member of the crew.

Smile, be honest, friendly and courteous. Don't ask questions. Look bored.

The customs guys all over the world are trained to use their sixth senses. If you're tired from the trip and harried by the hassle of mooring in a strange place you may give odd responses to them. Get some sleep before dealing with guys who are just doing a job. Clear into ports which "specialize" in yachts, or anchor around the corner with your yellow Q flag flying, and get a good night's sleep before entering.

FIREARMS

The most abused word among American yachties going south is "*confiscation*". I often meet disgruntled gun nuts headed north. Like Yosemite Sam, they wave their arms and stomp about and yell, "They CON-fiscated mah WEP'ns!"

All countries can hold onto your arms and even your bonded stores while you're in port, the US included. They may decline to check your arms depending on their own criteria such as the length of your stay, the length of your hair, security of your bonded locker and so on. The US, where military assault rifles are hawked on every street corner, doesn't bother. Puerto Rico usually won't. The USVI will, however.

If you sit long at a dock where gun-checking goes on, you shall rapidly become aware how some yachts carry enough arms to look like mercenaries out to overthrow the local government.

Finally, make sure your clearance-in papers are correct with respect to serial numbers and ammunition counts. If it's all checked on the way out and mistakes had been made, you're in for a major bureaucratic nightmare. Bullet counts are often off by one and corroded serial numbers are easily misread. Get it right on the way in.

BOAT AND DINGHY REGISTRATION

Vessels remaining in Puerto Rican waters more than 60 days must register in Puerto Rico. Fees are similar to Florida, e.g. a couple of hundred dollars for a 35-foot boat, plus registration for a dingy with a motor.

COMMUNICATIONS

MAIL

It is always best to use *general delivery*. Cafés, bars and marinas go out of business, change owners and policies. It is best to let the official postal system hold your mail for pickup. They are generally incorruptible, provide sorting and secure warehousing services which are their business. They are reasonably conscious of an obligation to you with respect to your mail. These things can not be said about a bar, restaurant or hotel where your mail will be pawed over by hundreds of cruisers, each one dripping wet and anxious to get to the bottom of the pile.

Your mail will be more conscientiously looked for by postal officials around the world if you follow this simple routine the first and every time you ask for it. Face the clerk squarely and look directly into his or her eyes. Smile brightly. Say "Good morning. How are you?" Pause and look like you're about to say good-bye, that you had only come there to make them happy. Then, with a shrug, remember you had minor business and, regretfully, wonder if they couldn't help you find your mail. Give them a card with your name written in large block letters. If your name is Van Somethingorother, tell them sometimes it's filed under Ess. This gambit works miracles everywhere. Even in the US Virgins.

In Puerto Rico use "General Delivery". Since PR is bilingual the clerk will be scanning for General Delivery not Lista de Correos after he sees your gringo face.

Reckon with US to Puerto Rico, four days. The USPO General Delivery.

HOW TO SEND THE MAIL

A tip about avoiding local taxes on parts shipped into Puerto Rico: send it *Priority Mail* or *Air Parcel Post* to *General Delivery* to small locations that have presort delivery. Examples are Boquerón, PR00622;

Salinas, PR00751; Fajardo, PR00740; or Culebra, PR00735. Uncle Sam refuses to collect local taxes, but large traffic points like San Juan, Mayagüez and Ponce have resident PR tax men who whomp you with 6.6% and delay delivery. Priority Mail may also help ensure delivery.

UPS is notoriously difficult for transients to deal with throughout the Caribbean.

Federal Express bends over backward to help in any way. FedEx is at 793-9300 in Puerto Rico. With FedEx you can call collect for pickup or inquiries to a *real person* who *can* answer your question. It may sound nautical to address yourself as:

—Captain John J. Courageous
—Aboard S/Y *Chicken Little*
—General Delivery

Your mail will almost certainly be stacked under <u>Captain</u>, or <u>Aboard</u>, or sent to the Little's household. Try this for better results:

—John Courageous
—General Delivery

Aside from the pretentiousness of such nautical addressing it makes you an easy mark. What do yacht people ever get except checks and bills? Their kids never write.

As you paw through the mail boxes yourself at the various bars and hotels along your route you will notice how nonuniform all those yachtie addresses are and how difficult they are to sort sensibly.

In Spanish countries, the middle name is often the main name for sorting. So leave out middle names unless you are John X. Smith.

TELEPHONE

It's usually easiest and cheaper to call collect or with credit card. You can dial direct from any street booth. Multiple use credit cards are on sale at many tourist locations for various denominations. It is also

11

possible to obtain telephone credit cards in the US without having a permanent home phone installation. You are billed according to usage, but there may be monthly limits, such as $100. This is sufficient for most cruisers unless, like Superman, they're running a business from the phone booths of the world.

The area code in Puerto Rico is 787 and the country code is the North American code: 1. If you start speaking in English they will answer you in English. The booths in Puerto Rico have instructions in English.

LANGUAGE

Don't let the myth of language barriers undo the enjoyment of your cruise.

I remember turning an aisle in a Caribbean supermarket. Across the room were two gaily dressed old geezers by the fruit shelves. They were waving at me. One had a camera around his neck. Half way across to them I realized they were a clever life-sized cardboard cutout advertising something. I felt quite follish. Most of us cruising the world see local life as these two dimensional cutouts unless, with luck, something occurs to get us involved. In non-English speaking countries, cruisers seldom get to read local newspapers. Uninterested in any subject outside their immediate yachtie environment, local language, newspapers, politics and so on lack reality and can't interest them.

In non-English speaking countries many cruisers excuse the lack of any but superficial interest with the old *language barrier*. Most, in fact, stay aboard waiting for weather rather than discover what's going on ashore or traveling inland. Many pay too much for everything and later whine they were "cheated". These cruisers never fulfill a good piece of their cruising goals.

With most of my adult life spent outside English speaking countries I think I have a qualified viewpoint on the matter. Simply put, *you erect your own language barriers*. Here's my experience. I have lived or worked in many countries where I did not speak the language. I have studied seven languages, and I came to live and work in four countries where I had to use the language well.

Yet I always got along *best* in the countries where I didn't know the language!

If you don't do the local language, people expect less of you and help you more. They have more patience with you, going out of their way to guide you. People are more interested in you. If you speak their language, you are more of an interloper in their society, not a visitor. Yes, humans practice prejudice everywhere. Parents show great interest when daughter brings the foreign exchange student home for dinner, but the excitement really gets big when she brings one home to marry! As a visitor not able to use the language at all, you have *privilege*. As a visitor trying to pick up a few words, you have sympathy, and honor as well.

If you seriously want to talk well in a foreign language, go ahead and make a serious try. Be prepared for a mind wrenching, personality bending experience. Yes, languages carry culture, and learning them requires personality change. Acquiring language often causes physical pain. It takes a long time and requires exhausting effort, yet it never can be 100% successful, despite what you've read in spy novels. It will give you great satisfaction, but it shall change forever your ability to be an interesting visitor everyone wants to help.

Get out and see the world while cruising, and don't erect your own language barriers. Wiggle your eyebrows, wave your arms, point to things and words and have fun, but don't ever say to me, "It's *easy* for you, you speak the language." That's precisely why it's not easy many times.

TRAVELING IN GROUPS

One of the nicest parts of cruising the Caribbean is that you see the same people again and again. Cruising in company, you can share your cocktail time with others. Headed south from Georgetown I've often been in company with from five-to-15 yachts. These trips weld friendships and make what is always a delightful trip south, even more enjoyable.

STAYING TOGETHER

One thing I always make clear to sailing companions is that I paddle my own canoe, do my own navigation, select my own anchorages, and when I grab a *weather window* and go, it's my own decision for my boat. I encourage everyone else to do likewise. My sailboat is my little universe on a savage sea, and she and I function as a team completely different from any other vessel and crew. This is no doubt true of all yachts and their crews. Unless there is an emergency at sea, we neither slow down to nor catch up with other boats, thus compromising the teamwork between crew and vessel,

and perhaps forcing an unnatural rhythm to her functioning at sea. I suspect many problems on the path south are precipitated by this phenomenon, and by the subconscious reliance on other boats. (*Well, if I miss the weather, one of the other guys is sure to have it.*) Proper respect for the sea and your vessel come first, demonstrations of camaraderie, second. Sailing in company, get advance permission to dawdle or leap ports ahead. So, sail alone, even in company.

BUDDY CHANNELS

Many boats sailing in company stay tuned to a "buddy channel" instead of VHF Channel 16. I have seen one yacht sunk and many others suffer narrow escapes while the "buddy boats" blithely sailed on in ignorance of repeated warnings on Channel 16.

FLEET OPERATIONS

One method of group cruising is to emulate a loose confederation of sovereign states. After all consultations are done, each captain must make his or her own decision, sharing it with the others out of courtesy, but not for approval. That's not to say, of course, that you can't change a decision upon hearing a wiser one made by someone else. Contact is maintained by radio and by common experiences in port.

If you are bound to stay together, then emulate the fascists whose emblem was the Roman *faces*, or bound bundle of spars. Appoint someone Navigator and someone else Admiral of the Fleet and make them responsible for putting voice to consensus. Democracy at sea can be dangerous. Picture a fleet of neophyte cruisers at sea, all strung out like a gaggle of geese, asking each other

on the VHF whether to reef or tack while assuring each other of their like-mindedness, regardless of each vessel's differences. I see them every year. Each boat thinks another boat is leading. The one in the lead doesn't know he's leading. He thinks he made a wrong tack and left the group. Whinnie The Pooh, off to discover the north pole, was better organized than most cruising groups I've heard on the VHF. Committee decisions, without a chairman to promulgate them wind up not being made at all. In port, preparing for a storm, that can be dangerous. *At sea it is purely deadly.*

SECURITY

Tales of Caribbean rape and pillage have titillated youngsters since the 1600's when the maraudings of L'Olenois, the *Corsaire*, and Morgan, the Privateer, first hit the British bookstalls. Many cruisers are adventurers and, to some extent, children, at heart. Their titillation runs wild upon occasion and their stories of piracy and skullduggery are among the many false dangers.

PERSONAL SECURITY

There are bad actors all over the world. Pirates are just bad guys potting at targets of opportunity upon the wastes of the sea, or in the alleys of the waterfronts. You're not in the Sulu Sea or the Red Sea, however. Your chances of running into a pirate in the Caribbean is even less than your chances of stumbling into one off Key Biscayne. Ask any European and you'll discover that most of the civilized world thinks America is among the most violent nations on the planet. Unfortunately, there is much to substantiate that opinion. Your exposure to personal assault, on your boat or ashore, is less almost anywhere in Puerto Rico than it is in any yachting center in the United States. Having said that, there are yet some caveats which may make for a more pleasant cruise.

SECURITY AFLOAT

Avoid pickup crew. The Caribbean is full of hitchhikers, both American and European, especially in the large yachting centers. Some are simply doing what used to be called *Le Grand Tour* between college and the start of a career. Others are simply doing you. If, after thorough investigation, you do take someone aboard, hold the person's passport and enough of his or her money to fly them back to their native country from your boat's destination. An even better filter of their real intentions is to do like the South Africans and some Europeans. Charge the crew for their room and board and the trip. Let the leeches pay or go get their own boat. Unbelievable folly has been met with pickup crew.

Avoid casual tours of your boat. What a thrill for that nice school girl to see a yacht. But she goes to school with not so nice school boys. A yacht has been a remote concept for them, unassailable as the homes of the local rich. Innocent talk at school, God forbid a fullblown Show and Tell, may make your snug little home familiar and assailable.

In anchorages without normal VHF traffic, leave your VHF on at night. It's your telephone. This may sound silly, but don't let anyone board your boat at any time for any reason unless they present indisputable documentation of their right to do so. Have deadlock bolts inside below, lock yourself in and wail on any radio frequency you can find.

Beware of *asymmetrical* cruisers. There are hustlers in the Caribbean without apparent resources and with hollowstories that don't fit neatly with accent, age, physiognomy, boat's and personal appearances. Yachties took turns inviting to dinner a good looking young fellow who had run out of funds. "And just imagine!" they gushed at me, "He's off around the world with no charts, no navigation aids and hardly a dime. What spirit! A real nice guy." He looked like a leech to me. After he'd left for the wide world, a rash of burglaries occurred while everyone was at a potluck. It was blamed on the locals. One yacht claimed a $10,000 loss and quit cruising. Mr. nice guy turned up in Central America fully equipped, saying he'd got the stuff cheap in Manzanillo. *Manzanillo?* I met rafts of cruisers down islands who still thought he was a great guy, and they were sincerely glad he had found the right equipment to go round the world. Aren't all con artists great guys?

SECURITY ASHORE

City waterfronts everywhere are close to rundown sections with poorer, sometimes desperate, inhabitants. Walking alone down unlit streets with flamboyant tourist garb, a bulging hip pocket and half a bag on from some happy hour isn't smart. In Cumaná, Venezuela, you're dead meat. Bracelets and necklaces are best left behind. You may know it's only costume jewelry, but does a 12 year old gutter snipe with a razor? Literal cutpurses running through a crowd in Caracas can bisect the strap on those belly bags yachties wear, neatly slicing your kidney in the bargain. It's happened.

On the other hand, it's not always so grim in the third world. It used to be that in Puerto Plata and Belize City, a naked sixteen year old virgin with fistfuls of dollars would attract only admiration. And you should have seen the alleys of Belize City at night in 1981. Times have been hard throughout the developing world. Skullduggery is up everywhere, perhaps even Puerto Rico. Until you know for sure, act as prudently as you would at home. No more nor less.

Instead of a wallet or purse, carry a sheet of paper with every number you ever needed, credit cards, telephones, citizenship, clearances, passports, whatever. Then wrap your folding walking around money over your credit card and slip it into a flapped pocket.

Squid

15

BOAT SECURITY

There are as few anchorages in the Caribbean where I feel I must lock up my boat as there are towns in America where one can leave one's doors open. Most places, if a local inhabitant breaks through your locks he'll cause more loss through damage to teak joinery than he will through the trinkets he's likely to walk off with.

Only boaties take boaty things. Remember that when you anchor next to the dirtbag boat full of hippies in a lonely cove. Such "cruisers" do exist in the Caribbean. Avoid these boats and their crews. If they need a snatch block they'll snatch yours. But that's rare in the Caribbean unless you are in the wrong place to begin with.

How and where you moor the boat when you are away from it will provide you with more insurance than any insurance company or commercial guard service can offer. During extended absences, unless you can put up in a guarded marina, securely anchor the boat in a weather safe anchorage, far enough from young swimmers from the shore, near enough to be seen by the casual observer, and in amongst other yachts whose owners you know and trust. Leave them instructions for access to the boat as well as for charging the battery, feeding the parakeet or what-all else.

Alarm systems, like those in suburban America, turn in more false alarms than real. But if you're a gadgeteer and have the money, by all means, have the fun of installing them and spoofing your friends with all the hooting of horns and strobing of lights. Any local intruder, not knowing what to expect, is likely to think that this display is all quite normal boat behavior. One boater I know has a neat switch over his bunk. When he throws it, a brilliant flood light mounted high forward in the saloon blinds anyone in the cockpit, the companion way, or messing about inside. Like a stun grenade: effective, simple and cheap.

FIREARMS

If you have firearms, be trained in their use and know when to use them. Never brandish a firearm. If you take one in hand it should be to use it. It's use is not to scare but to kill. Pretty serious stuff. Firearms aboard can be a hassle while clearing in and out.

The problem lies in threat assessment. Sober, nonprejudicial judgment is necessary. But that's rarely possible in a strange, poverty stricken land, where people speak a different language with excited jabbers and ominous overtones. It's certainly difficult when you're roused out of a sound evening cocktail induced slumber after a long, hard, adrenaline drenched beat to weather by an undercover narcotics agent. Impulsive resort to a firearm is invitation to tragedy. Probably yours.

DINGHY SECURITY

If you haven't learned dinghy security in the US waters, here's some tips to help you. Motor and dinghy theft is not a problem where locals with a yacht dinghy would stand out like a dugout canoe in a Connecticut yacht club. Theft will occur where there is a ready market for either the motor or the dinghy.

First, use chain or coated stanless cable of minimum size 5/16", with a minimum of 12 feet. Chain is better. Padlock or permanently secure the chain to a permanent steel fitting attached to a hard surface of the dink (transom, for instance), _not_ the towing eye of an inflatable dinghy — thieves will simply cut them off. I know of one case in where

is your alarm system and enables you to catch the varmint in the act and while still in the water. Depending on the sternness of your response, you won't have trouble at that anchorage for the rest of your stay. I've found flare guns neatly scare everyone in the anchorage as well as the varmint, and they certainly light up the scene of the crime well and call the attention of any law enforcement which may be around and pretending not to notice. Flares also continue to burn in the water, catching the crook in a ring of light.

If I'm concerned about a dinghy thief in the night, I leave my stern light on (it's separately wired), a cockpit anchor light on, and I have a cutlass and a flare pistol handy. Once I squeezed intersecting streams of

they cut off the transom. Even if your motor is locked securely onto the transom, run the chain through the motor handle as well. Finally, lock the chain to some permanent fixture ashore with an eye to tide and current. You may want an anchor out to keep from sawing against a pier or going under one at low tide. If you don't, you may come back to a crushed motor when the tide rises.

Lock your dinghy to the boat, coiling excess chain in a bunch on deck so it doesn't go overboard unless pulled upon. The thunk, thunk, thunk of the links going over the rail

muriatic acid and ammonia from their squirt bottles. The effect was devastating to the machete wielding bandit in the water. A friend prefers a "wrist rocket" sling shot with ball bearings. One fellow I know brought back a blowgun from South America with some pretty serious darts. I've thrown rocks from the cat toilet for double insult.

If you have big motorized davits, use them to haul up your dinghy and motor every night. Another method is to arrange a three-point bridle with its lifting ring centered to keep the raised dinghy and motor level as you haul the rig up to the rail with your halyard. Make the bridle out of stainless cable, or it may be chopped readily with a machete.

Plaster your dinghy and motor with reflective tape so you can find it when it drifts away at night. It also becomes a less attractive target for thieves. An inflatable in the Virgin Islands becomes less attractive to thieves (other boaters), if it is plastered with multicolored patches and 5200. One of my best dinghy trades was a flawless Avon RIB that looked like it had been through the battle of Trafalgar. I never had to lock that one up.

Finally, at crowded dinghy docks, leave your dink anchored well off with thirty or so feet of painter run to the dock. Neophyte cruisers often snug their painters to the dock and tip their motors up. As the tide changes their props become bucking and slashing scythes which will cut your bow section to ribbons. I usually make a dinghy dock with a stern anchor out, actually an undeployed grapnel. A rock can do as well. I land perpendicularly to the dock a distance down from where I want the painter tied. The dinghy then lays off roughly that same distance, well free of the crowd. It can be retrieved at any point by dragging, since the anchor, or rock, isn't grabbing hard.

ANCHORING IN THE CARIBBEAN

Many folks who have sailed a bunch have not anchored much, though they may think they have, myself included, until they get to the Caribbean, especially by short hops. I spent some time interviewing a family who had sailed 15,000 miles round the world in three years to end it all on the Cayos Caribes, motoring to a waypoint given to them with great care and precision by a "friend"; a waypoint inside the cut itself. They had anchored less than a dozen times in three years. They took long legs and hung out for long periods to refresh their kitty when they stopped.

ARE YOU A GOOD NEIGHBOR?

The best neighbor in an anchorage is the one that's silent while you are anchoring or weighing anchor. Let the new boat anchor in peace. I sometime get gratuitous complaints that I'm too close to someone's boat while I start to lay my first anchor. Then the guy sees the second anchor deployed and my boat lays on a wide vee 100 feet off his quarter.

Anglophones particularly worry about comFrancophones whose sensitivity radius is much smaller than theirs. I personally prefer Latin closeness to Anglo aloofness. Anyway, Anglos have a perception problem. The French may anchor closer, but I notice they do a good job of it, if not better. *Charter*phones are feared by all, and with good reason.

A good neighbor does not call you on the radio nor dinghy over to talk to you while you are in the act of anchoring or weighing anchor. Sometimes I go to the shortest possible scope, hoist the mainsail, then haul anchor before she starts to drag. People sometimes dinghy over to meet me just as a gust takes the sail and the boat starts to move. I try to be friendly while maneuvering under sail in a crowded anchorage, but I'm afraid I sound rude. Isn't it better to get to know each other during all the days together in harbor?

A good neighbor doesn't offer help or advice unless asked. I take my time. I don't strain myself or my boat. Sometimes it's a two-cupper: two cups of coffee to let the chop unglue the anchor while I flake the chain out to dry. Once a guy they called "Animal" stormed aboard uninvited. He dashed up to the bow where I was one-handedly plucking a few slack links, coffee in the other hand. "Here!" he shouted, shoving me aside, "Let me show you how to put some *ass* in that thing." While I was still trying to figure out what hit me, he popped the anchor up right through the teak grating on the bowsprit. Satisfied, he hopped back into his dinghy beside his admiring surfer girl and sped off, waving at me with a big grin, while *Jalan Jalan*, untimely loosed, drifted broadside toward a pier with her bowsprit platform in splinters.

BRIDGE COMMUNICATIONS

This is a subject that ought to be under a heading of *Marriage Counseling*. Mom and Pop on their retirement cruise have never been so close for so long in forty years. Now they're farthest apart only while they're anchoring. And that's only thirty feet or so.

Pop stands at the wheel because he's so technical, while Mom stands at the bow anchor because she's got stronger hands. Some prefer to reverse the roles. One or the other signals and the miscommunication begins.

It can take another 40 years to develop hand signals and the concomitant divided responsibilities which are needed to choreograph the delicate ballet of anchoring successfully in all conditions and in front of the usual audiences who are pretending to look the other way. If you can't do it alone at least follow these rules.

The bowman (-woman) should do all signaling from the same position always and with the same hand always while holding the forestay with the other hand to ensure its immobility even more than to ensure bowman's stability. Signals needed are:

left	center-wheel	ahead
hard-left	astern	power-up
right	power-down	stop
hard-right	@^$*%>#!!!	

Setting or weighing anchor is always easiest before or after the trades blow.

The last command is optional but preserves harmony in the more untested relationships. Roadman signals work fine. So do crane operator signals.

To avoid nasty equivocation keep all fingers together.

To really do it right get one of those walkie talkies on headsets. You can build them into beanies with the boat's name on them. That way they can't be seen by the audience who will think you're just plain proficient.

One couple I saw do this really looked great while silently anchoring with this advanced communications equipment. At least until Pop suddenly screamed at Mom from the bow, apparently apropos of nothing, "I said starboard, dammit!"

LAYING ANCHOR

Yachts that drag into you in the tight anchorages invariably seem to pay more attention to sailing than to seamanship. Ninety-five percent of seamanship lies in the art of *keeping the boat from moving* and only five percent in making it go. Below are some aphorisms which, taken together, go a bit toward describing the art of anchoring.

§ **Don't anchor near boats with damaged topsides.**

§ **Don't anchor near boats with performance hulls or rigs.**

Chances are they are five-percenters and have only five feet of chain. They dance all over the harbor in any breeze. I watched one hull-sailing full circles all night long. He had two anchors, thank goodness, and the boat wound itself down like a cuckoo clock and took off on the other tack for another fifteen circles.

§ **Small boats (under 50') are best anchored by one person.**

In this way one person will know what was done at the time of anchoring and the knowledge will not reside somewhere between the wheel and the pulpit with neither station actually being responsible. This rule can save marriages as well.

Preparing the boat to fall off in the proper direction before laying the anchor is best the responsibility of the person who selects the spot and lays the anchor, not someone at the helm who doesn't quite know where the spot is or how the anchor may soar to it. It also calls for knowledge of the boat's char-

vert to kind and plow a furrow. Watch for drag by picking a range (not other boats) perpendicular to the extended rode. Also, a grasped rode can telegraph dragging to your hand. If the wind is up, it may be difficult to set even a Danforth in mangrove mud or hard marl. In a wind, you shall have to motor forward at low revs so as to maintain slow enough sternway to permit the anchor to set.

acteristics of way, its momentum, and how easily she faces or crosses the wind.

While anchoring single-handedly, however, it is essential that the maneuver to station the slowly swinging bow over the spot selected be well timed to enable the walk forward from the helm to the pulpit to be accomplished with a certain seamanlike decorum, rather than a headlong, cursing rush.

§ **Set anchors by wind and current first**

Not by someone behind eighty horses unable to see what's happening, unless there is no wind or current. Burying types such as Bruces and plows, dig in by wiggling and worming with the action of the sea and tug of the chain. If you apply full tractor power to them before they've hooked, they will re-

§ **Anchors are to be *laid*, not dropped, thrown or swung**

Laying an anchor implies touching its crown to the bottom, gently *laying* its biting side down, and allowing a smooth backward drift in the direction of the expected flow of wind or current, while *laying* the chain in a straight line behind the straightly *laid* anchor. *Lay* enough chain to ensure pull on the anchor will be directed along the bottom, which you gently hook. Pay out more rode and dig it in harder. Repeat and test with motor. Sailors who routinely talk about <u>dropping the hook</u>, you will find, often have hooks instead of proper anchors and usually simply <u>drop</u> them, heavily trussed in a bundle of rope and chain.

§ Select anchors for bottom and boat

All anchors benefit by being properly laid, especially Fortress and Bruce types.

§ Come to rest before paying out tackle

Pay out the final bit of scope, or, as the case may be, snug it in, only after securing the yacht and tidying up the deck. That will ensure more time for her to reach rest condition. The seaman who takes longest to get his yacht settled on her anchors is probably the sailor doing the best job of anchoring.

§ Dive on the anchor to check it

If necessary, set it by hand. While you are down there check your neighbors' as well. I was cruising in company with a good friend who is a professional diver on the oil rigs. In deference to his skills and my taste I started on the SG&Ts while he dived on the anchors. He found a neighbor's anchor lying sideways on the bottom. "Impossible!" shouted the salty-whiskered downeaster while posed cross-armed and bantam-like on his taffrail. "I set that anchor with 55 horses!" My friend set the fellow's anchor for him in order to protect our own boats.

Use about a pound of anchor for every foot of the boat. A 45 pound Danforth would suit a 41 foot boat, but not as a single anchor if wind or current can switch. Danforths, while capable of tremendous holding power, do not reset themselves well and the stock can go afoul. Heavy burying type anchors such as the CQR or Bruce work well on almost all bottoms and tend to reset themselves. They don't foul as easily as Danforth types. Use Danforth types in mud or grassy bottoms, making well sure the points are dug in. In a blow, Danforths hold best pound for pound. No matter what the Danforth folks say, don't use a short length of chain. It may function in theory but, in the Caribbean, any nylon rode less than one inch shall most cetainly chafe through on the bottom, if not by coral, then by broken rum bottles.

§ For rocky bottoms use a heavy prayer.

§ Use enough chain:
long enough and *big* enough

Consider first that the chain's catenary must never be able to reach the anchor itself so as to exert upward drag on the shank — even in the most violent conditions — *especially* in the most violent conditions. Second, ensure that any rode attached cannot come into contact with the seabed or obstructions on it (coral heads, rocks, wrecks and broken rum bottles).

You might consider including enough chain so that chafe at deck level does not occur, i.e., all chain. Also, the catenary of an all chain rode makes a good shock absorber. If you use all chain, attach a nylon rode snubber as long as necessary to quiet the action. Absolute minimum chain length should be five feet for every sixteenth of an inch of chain size, i.e., 25 feet for 5/16 chain, 30 feet for 3/8, etc. An alternate rule of thumb is to use between 1 and 1 1/2 boat lengths.

For full displacement boats, add a sixteenth of an inch in chain size for every ten feet of boat's length above 20 feet. Thus, for LOA's 20-29 feet use 5/16", for 30-39 feet use 3/8", for 40-49 feet use 7/16", and for 50-59 feet use 1/2".

For all chain use a scope of three to five times the depth of water <u>added to the distance from sea level to anchor roller</u>.

For chain and rode use a scope five to seven times the depth <u>added to the distance from sea level to anchor roller</u>.

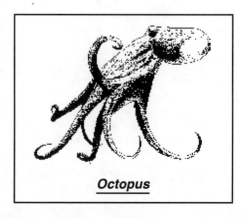

Octopus

21

To reduce the amount of scope required in tight anchorages, consider extending your anchor snubbers from a bow eye at the water line.

To reduce vertical snatching loads on the bow, buoy the rodes before leading them to the bow.

§ Consider using two anchors

The actual uses of the Bahamian Moor, one anchor against each expected change of current direction, are few: tidal bays, coves, creeks or rivers. These are places where currents can be strong and regularly reverse with the tide.

Nine out of ten of your anchorages will be in harbors or against beaches where these effects are minimal. So why use two anchors?

Because everyone around you does and if you don't you'll find your bow poking into someone's bedroom in the middle of the night.

Because you expect a switch in the wind or a front to come; or worse, because you *don't* expect it.

Because your harbor goes absolutely calm at night and you want to prevent the boat from walking around your lone anchor, droodling chain all over and under it, so that when the morning wind rises you drag onto the beach, towing a ball of tackle.

Because you're the first one in harbor and you expect 40 other partying boaters to plunk balls of chain all around you in the middle of the night and you want to keep your elbows tucked in.

Because you don't want to wind your rode around a coral head.

Because you're in the anchorage for the first time and aren't quite sure about that wide open fetch to the Southwest.

Because you're leaving the boat unattended.

BUT, if everyone else is swinging on one anchor, go with the flow and set only one yourself so they don't bash you.

WEIGHING ANCHOR

The following may seem old hat. But sit any morning in harbor and watch the scene while folks up anchors. Before observing too long, you'll want a tot of rum in your coffee.

§ When weighing anchor,
keep the chain *vertical*

Doing this ensures two things. First you will approach the anchor along the chain's lie and in a pace commensurate with safety and the proper stowing of the tackle. Secondly, you are unlaying the links of chain right up to the anchor's shank, ensuring that you don't dislodge the anchor until ready and it won't skitter and roil around the seabed fouling things like other people's rodes.

The chain can be kept vertical under the bow by:

— never powering beyond the catenary, instead let the catenary pull the yacht forward, not the coronary, and— using the windlass only to pull up slack links, not to pull the yacht.

So: when walking the yacht up her ground tackle: *let the 'canary' pull it.*

§ Keep station until it clears the water

The bane of all anchorages is the morning clod who, upon sensing the anchor has broken loose, turns his head aft and yells "She's up!", and off the yacht drifts downwind, with a giant grappling hook beneath her soaring a few inches off the bottom, headed almost surely for your rode. Even bane-ier is the knucklehead who powers about the anchorage with an acute angle of chain stretched behind the bow while the crew tries to wrestle up the taut chain and anchor before they snag — you guessed it — *your rode!*

PROVISIONING AND REPAIRS

Do major provisioning in the Walmart, Pueblo and Cash and Carry stores on Route 3 just north of the town of Fajardo. Anchor or take a slip at Isleta and shuttle with the Isleta Ferry to Puerto Real where publicos run frequently to Fajardo. *Publicos* also run frequently between Fajardo and the major malls outside on the highway. A more convenient and, in the long run, perhaps a more economic alternative is to put up at Puerto del Rey Marina and hire a car for a day.

In Fajardo bolt ends and reject lengths of Sunbrella can be had at *Cien Almecenes* at the northwest corner of the square.

While shopping on Route 3 do lunch or dinner at *Lolita's*, the best (and most reasonable) Mexican restaurant in Puerto Rico. Across from *Lolita's* is the best deal on Imron paint at a store whose sign reads "*pintula*". Paint in Spanish is *pintura*, but Puerto Ricans often slur their r's into l's, thus the spelling *pintula*.

Sail repair and several good marine and fishing stores are at Villa Marina. You can reach Villa Marina by gofast dinghy from Isleta, or bring the big boat in and lay alongside for the visit.

Starfish

Puerto Rico's east coast has good haul-out facilities, and good marine stores. For major work, however, you shall eventually travel to hunt things down in San Juan, launching epic travails and travels. St. Thomas may beckon if the job seems beyond the resources of Fajardo. Not a bit! The USVIs don't have Puerto Rico's industrial economy, something necessary to support a tough boat job. Industrial strength support is on the south coast, however.

Serious jobs which don't require haulout, such as installing a water maker or auto pilot, are best attacked by taking the boat around to Salinas on the South coast. Salinas is a safe and commodious harbor in which to decommission the boat for extended work, or for wet storage.

Larry's Playa Marine on the Salinas anchorage has the best stainless stock in Puerto Rico, and just about anything else you can think of.

In nearby Ponce is the most amazing warehouse you'll ever visit: Rubber and Gasket of Puerto Rico (843-8450), which has sheet rubber, Teflon, Lexan, and any kind of hose you want, including stainless flex. And they fabricate. Everything can be had in Ponce. Stainless fabrication is at Accurate Tooling (AT Metal) on Hostos in Playa Ponce. Owner Luis Ojeda is also Commodore of the Ponce Yacht Club. Near the yacht club is Benitez Carrillo, a dealer that has vee belts, bearings, gears, seals, motor controls and every ball bearing known to man, even your roller furling's.

CASH

Cash is available in most major tourist centers with American Express cards at any American Express office, and VISA and Master Charge at most commercial banks, including automatic teller machines.

If you carry a lot of cash, don't flash a roll. Keep it in separate pockets. Purses and "belly bags" have been known to get ripped off in some areas of the Caribbean.

FUEL AND WATER

Water should be taken on whenever available. Always bleach water with 1 tablespoon bleach per 30 gallons of water. Treat your water with chlorine and never tank from a line after a recent loss of pressure.

Always filter the fuel with a Baja Filter if you can get it, tee shirts if you can't. (The Baja Filter is a California invention for use in cruising the Baja. It is a funnel which has nested, removable filters of successively finer mesh through which fuel is poured into the tank. The best will have a Teflon coated filter to separate water as well.)

One year I had five motor stops at sea due to clogged fuel filters. Another time, I bucketed out all the fuel from the tank and gleaned four pounds of sand and gravel.

FOODS

avocado	aguaca-te	banana	guineo	breadfruit	buen pan	key limes	limones
plantain	plátano	cashew	cajuil	chayote	tayota	cocoa	cacao
coffee	café	grapefuit	toronja	guava	guaya-ba	manioc	yuca
mango	mango	passion fruit	chinola	orange	naranj-a	papaya	lechosa
peanuts	maní	pear	pera	pineapple	piña	potato	papa
sapodilla	zapote	sour sop	guaya-bana	sweet potato	batata	tomato	tomate

WHAT TO BUY

First of all, only you know what you want. I love French cut green beans and I use them with mushrooms, onions and mayonnaise for great salads when I can't get fresh veggies. You may hate French cut green beans and mushrooms.

FRESH FRUITS AND VEGETABLES

The same should be said for fresh veggies as was said for fuel and water: buy them whenever they're available. And wash them before putting them aboard. Also be sure to take away all cardboard which may bring aboard cockroach eggs.

Get to the markets early. Often you shall find varying quality in all the little shops and on the streets. Find the lady that has the best of what you want, then find out when she gets it in fresh. Try out the different root vegetables that fed our ancestors before the Idaho white potato and mass production methods drove them from North America.

DRY STAPLES

Have smallish dry staple containers aboard. Rice, sugar, flour, beans, meal, and so on, are readily available almost everywhere and at reasonable prices.

Trying to store too much flour or rice will have you throwing it away when the insect eggs hatch, that is, unless you have pounds of Laurel (bay leaves) to put in your canisters. You may need to clean the rice and beans of small stones and stems. When visiting Florida I found myself cleaning a bag of beans as was my Caribbean habit. After discarding more than usual the amount of small dirt clods and sticks, I was surprised to see it was a bag I had bought in the U.S. So much for superior food standards.

While giant stateside supermarkets abound in Puerto Rico, so do small grocery stores or *colmados*. Here you may find Caribbean products in which flour is not always "enriched", rice is not always "polished", sugar is not always "refined" and not much is "new and improved". But it just might be tasty and good for you.

BREAD

Bakeries or *panaderias*, are ubiquitous in Spanish countries where they make fresh *pan del agua* ("Cuban" or small French breads) twice a day.

MEATS AND SAUSAGES

You will often get tough and tasteless beef in restaurants and in stores and conclude that meat is awful, a complaint often heard from yachties who just didn't know what to order and how.

Cheap beef is called *res* [race] and is often tough. The secret to buying good meat is to not go cheap. Buy the most expensive filet, *filete* [fee-LAY-taye] *lomillo* [low-ME-yo], and you will be very pleased. *Solomillo* [SO-low-ME-yo] is sirloin. Local smoked ham, boiled ham and smoked pork chops are also good.

If you can, get a *Saronno* ham to hang aboard. This is the Spanish version of the Italian Parma ham.

CANS

I have fished cans out of the forward bilge after three years aboard in the tropics and found them still legibly labeled and delicious inside. Varnishing cans is a waste of time if yours is a basically dry boat.

EGGS

I've had unrefrigerated eggs aboard as long as two months and found them delicious, although they don't foam as much when whipped if you don't turn them. Of course, you must buy only unrefrigerated, fresh eggs; refrigerated eggs go bad quicker. Unrefrigerated eggs are easy to spot. They have chicken poop on them. Instead of waxing your eggs, try turning them once in a while to keep the yolks centered. Like many cruising customs of yore, modern yachts and ubiquitous staples eliminate varnishing tins and waxing eggs.

STREET FOOD

I know I've got it coming to me, but going on 30 years living abroad in the strangest of places, I've been ill from food just twice. Once was a long time ago at the grand restaurant of the Palace Hotel in Biarritz. In India, one would expect to become ill from the *nazi* balls (rice balls) the peddler rolls in his hands and pops into ancient hot grease. Not so. Perhaps the super hot oil does it. Latin countries have superb little puffed, stuffed pastries (*empanadillas* in Puerto Rico).

HAULING OUT

Puerto Rico is dotted with boatyards. You will have no trouble finding one for a quick haul and paint. For more extensive work, as always, shop around before committing.

If leaving your boat for the summer, consider hauling out and leaving it at Ponce Yacht Club (expensive), or Palmas del Mar, near Humacao, or *Puerto del Rey*, in Fajardo. *Puerto del Rey* is the largest marina in the Caribbean and very well equipped, though it can be dear, depending.

Croabas, Puerto Real and Isleta have little or no facility for long term storage but are good and fast haulouts. At Palmas del Mar, your boat can be laid up either ashore or afloat and the yard has a marine store with yard owner Hans Grossen as helpful as he can be. Las Croabas is do-it-yourself and usually cheapest.

NAVIGATION AIDS

Most cruisers are consumed with getting to a certain place at a certain time. For this they heavily invest in all sorts of navigational equipment. The real art of navigation, however, is to not be in the wrong place at the wrong time. This should be your criterion for choosing navigational aids.

CHARTS

NOAA charts 25650, 25653, 25668, 25677 and 25687. These are available in yachting versions in most marine stores as Waterproof Charts from International Marine Supply, or in Imray charts which offer the scale a yachtsman is interested in, showing landmarks of interest to the small boat skipper making for small harbors. Bluewater Books & Charts of Ft. Lauderdale also has one of the country's most comprehensive inventories of charts and guides for all of the Caribbean and other regions.

Both these charts have formats which better fit small boat nav tables than do DMA or NOAA charts, and they have color contrasts.

PILOT CHARTS

I keep a pilot chart on my chart table at all times. It is used only occasionally for plotting Caribbean crossings, tracking Tropical Storms. and planning passages with the current and wind data it provides. However, it is used every morning in the Bahamas to plot the Cold Fronts and every morn-ing in the Caribbean to plot the Tropical Waves. It is the single most used chart aboard and is covered with pencil marks and coffee rings. The best buy the US Government ever offered is the chart table sized book of twelve *Pilot Charts of the Central American Waters* at the price of only one regular chart.

ALMANACS

These are of great use as reference works aboard. (What *is* the breaking strength of 5/16 BBB chain, anyway?) I have found that a single copy of *Reed's Nautical Almanac* from any year provides more useful information than *Chapman's* and *Bowditch's* combined.

TIDE TABLES

In the English Channel I was never without my tide tables and current guides. The tides were, after all, 34 feet at my moorings, and the currents reached 9 knots! In the Caribbean there's nothing to know outside the information on the Pilot Charts which doesn't vary year to year.

None of this is really necessary, however, since most places you can assume high tide *is at 8 o'clock* local time everywhere near open sea *on the day of a* full moon. So you can add 52 minutes a day thereafter and do without tide tables.

NOTE: The south side of the Greater Antilles and the Virgin Islands have diurnal tides with a higher high and a lower low instead of two lows and two highs.

SMALL SCALE CHARTS

These charts cover large geographical areas. They make great wall decorations at home; at sea, I have only those needed to plot crossings and major passages.

THE BARE MINIMUM

COMPASS

I had sailed for years with no more than a compass and a log. After cruising a while I found that even the log was a luxury. Knowledge of your boat's speed settles into your bones after only a few weeks of cruising. You can navigate surely and safely forever with only a compass by careful and frequent position plotting, attention to leeway, current and tidal currents, and by introducing intentional errors in order to ensure which side of a feature you make your landfall. Even the compass needn't be all that accurate, since who can hold a perfect course anyway, what with all that bobbing around?

Old fashioned binnacles look nice and are useful for taking bearings of ships. But, they are rarely visible from comfortable positions while seated. Your compass should be mounted where you can see it comfortably from your sailing position on either tack while cruising. Bolt upright behind or beside the wheel is a racing position. The cruising steering position has a little more Zen in it. For instance, I sail scrunched up in a ball in the same corner of the cockpit on both tacks, never behind the wheel. Therefore I use a bulkhead compass.

The compass should have a large, legible scale which is well illuminated, not just bright. Some compass lights illuminate everything but the card's scale. Ideally you should have a compass which is rapidly damped. This usually means a larger and more expensive model, but not always.

Swing your compass from time to time,

even if it's compensated, to confirm your compass' deviation table, and make sure you are using this year's variation.

LOG

Mechanical sumlogs, taffrail log, or any device which keeps a digital track of miles run is a great check on the navigator. They all fail, however, and there is no substitute for the skipper knowing intuitively how fast his yacht is going through the water.

Before the impeller is tangled in seaweed or a shark eats the rotor, take the time to calibrate your sense of the boat's speed by the old chip log method. Select a fixed length of deck viewed from your sailing position. Time bits of foam passing between perpendiculars of that length, checking results with actual speedo readings. Speed in knots is twice the meters travelled divided by the seconds taken.

$$\frac{2 \times \text{Meters}}{\text{seconds}}$$

Practice makes perfect and eventually you will know with a glance how fast your boat is going in all conditions. It is an old principle of navigation that the more regular and frequent your plots are, the more sure your course. Without a sumlog, plotting intervals should become shorter. This is due to the fact that you have got to estimate average speed over the last interval and, the shorter the interval, the more accurate your estimate shall be.

SEXTANT

The last time I used my sextant was crossing the Atlantic in 1979. In the Bahamas and the Caribbean they're only useful if you really know how to use them on clear and starry nights. I have a friend who is able to pull off a three-star fix faster than my Satnav could prepare one, and be just as accurate (he can't beat a GPS). Solar and lunar sights, however, don't usually provide the kind of precision required to navigate among islands. If you are island hopping, the distances are not great and landfalls are unmistakable and inevitable in the Caribbean. On the other hand, if you are crossing the Caribbean Sea, or you are masochistically beating over the ocean to St.Thomas, great accuracy isn't really called for, but the sextant can be useful to confirm drift. I'm afraid sextants have gone the way of the slide rule. Still, they're neat. Every skipper should have one to play with.

Your time and money is better spent on chart work and a good compass. You don't want to be like the "professional" delivery crew who gave up their charge on East Reef, Mayaguana, having spent all their time playing with their sextants and none of it on avoiding a lee reef. The day after the paid crew of three deserted their ship, by the way, it was taken off the reef whole by one salvor using the boat's own ground tackle. He turned the key and motored off with the boat.

ELECTRONIC NAVIGATION AIDS

Safety at sea is not bought with expensive equipment nor fancy calculations. Both are subject to operator error and other failures in a crisis. As Eric Hiscock was fond of saying, "The price of safety at sea is eternal vigilance".

If all you really need is a chart and a compass, then why spend the money on fancy electronic navigation aids? Well, the older I get, the mistakier I get. Once I missed the Dry Tortugas entirely because a pair of pliers left under the compass gave me a deviation of seventeen degrees.

hours we slowed our progress toward Exuma Sound, which, with only raging cuts to leeward, would be a deathtrap in those conditions, by zigzagging down breaking waves in continual darkness.

My oval of navigational uncertainty became so big, I still don't know if we passed the Plana Cays and the surrounding reefs on the west or the east. Three months later I had a Satnav on board.

In general, the more navigation aids, electronic or not, the better. Bless you for being affluent enough to afford them, clever enough to select the right ones from the welter of black boxes on the market, and patient enough to maintain them. Which devices will serve you the most on the way south? This list follows, like the last one, in priority order.

DEPTH SOUNDER

The depth sounder, or fathometer, is a much under-used tool among yachties. This navigation aid is only second to the compass. A reliable digital depthfinder in the cockpit is great for coasting. Tack in to 20 fathoms, tack out to 50, and so on. Additionally, there is some evidence that sounders left on, even when off soundings, deter broaching marlins and whales from coming up under the boat.

Finding your position off a coast where everything looks the same is child's play by using the Chain of Soundings method.

Chain of Soundings Method

This is a method of navigation that many of us use unconsciously while coasting in order to confirm the boat's position. With chart in hand, keep mental track of the soundings shown on the fathometer. If the readings of the fathometer do not agree with your expectations gained from the chart, you have reason to wonder where you really are.

By sailing a straight line and taking soundings at regular intervals one can arrive at a "signature" of the bottom which usually identifies only that line over that

Nature also makes mistakes, often enhanced by the bureaucracy. Each year there is a budgetary wrangle between the Air Force, NASA, and the Department of Commerce over hurricane surveillance responsibilities. It usually isn't resolved, but they begin to cooperate by late summer and cease abruptly on November 1st. If you don't believe it, watch the newspapers carefully as June 1 approaches.

December 19th, 1984, the NWS forecast continuing fine weather. We up-anchored and sailed for Georgetown from the north shore of Caicos. They came back 6 hours later with a hurricane warning for hurricane Lilly which they placed exactly 90 miles off my stern and blowing me northwest into the islands. *Lilly* was a small, tight 'cane, out of season and bearing no telltale feeder trails. She broke up early but spawned several days of gales throughout the area. *Lilly* was only a hiccup for Mother Nature, of no interest on Capitol Hill, but a major surprise to small boats.

When that hurricane forecast was received I was already on the run before it, surfing down ten footers with the log pegged at eight knots, and me, between curses, wondering what the heck was going on. For 36

29

bottom. A somewhat complex, but un-equivocal, way of doing it is to plot the readings to scale on a piece of clear plastic or tracing paper. Then move the tracing about on the chart until you have a match. Of course the bottom must vary, and sometimes the line is long and you have to get it all done before you've left the area and become lost again. As long as I am on soundings I prefer to just make mental note of the fathom lines as I cross them and never lose my chain of soundings in the first place.

VHF

VHF is required. Get an international switch and lots of channels. See *Using the Radio*.

AM/FM

Of course you have AM/FM aboard with cassette or CD player. You should also have a hand sized portable with a rod type extendable aerial in the emergency locker. If you have to abandon ship you can listen to all the religious stations that dot the Caribbean. But more important, you can use it as a highly reliable radio direction finder, homing in on island rock stations. Reception will be loudest when the aerial is perpendicular to the rhumb line to the station. Perhaps the combination of direction and religion will save you.

SSB RECEIVER

For following the National Weather Service reports and the various cruiser nets you must have a radio capable of receiving SSB. A cheap portable with a "BFO" switch which can receive the frequencies is usually sufficient. Before you pay $300 for a SONY look at more professional gear which may even be cheaper in the long run and give much better reception. I had two of those small portable units which corroded. One of the older, larger models, however, lasted for years.

GPS

They come in a variety of models. Cheap is best. You both save money and eliminate confusion during operation. All GPS units seem to have the worst human factors built into their consoles since spark advance was eliminated from steering wheels. "Hooboy!", says the engineer, "if we connect the freemis to the gizzis, and you press these six buttons at once, you'll get the Gregorian date expressed in hexidecimal." "Grrreat!" explodes the marketeer, and into the machine it goes.

The more expensive models are loaded up with inane "functional add-ons". These are do-hickeys the manufacturers make to keep up unit price in an expanding market. As an example consider 900 waypoints. Unless you're a fisherman or a smuggler on regular and complicated routes, you shouldn't need more than a few waypoints. Where you came from, where you're going (with a couple of options), a couple of real waypoints, and the location of a weather feature you may want range and bearing on. Leave one or two waypoints to play with and you've justified 10.

When road-based transportation installs GPS receivers *en masse*, then relatively low-cost, low-function units will be available to the yachtsman. Until then, they are expensive.

GPS Cautions

—Check every waypoint with charts when you enter it and adjust for sea room.

—While coasting, make your own fixes regularly by compass bearings and confirm with the GPS. This ensures your continuous recognition of land features.

—While planning or executing a crossing, keep estimated positions (EPs), not DRs (dead reckoning). EPs include current, leeway, tide, magnetic variation and magnetic deviation. Steering a straight line across the bottom may be the longest way to go for either sail or motor, especially in reversing tidal streams.

—Ignore entrance waypoints given by "helpful" yachties down to the hundredth of a mile (20 yards). The future shall see many yachts motored onto reefs while headed to an entrance or sea buoy waypoint. Get out your chart. Step up to a mile off of the entrance, and make that your waypoint, from where you will go on visual.

A yachtie took his dinghy to the little red ball inside one of my reefed entrances. Holding his hand on the buoy, he took several GPS readings and averaged them. Next morning he called southbound yachts on the SSB. Proud as Columbus, he told them of his venture with the "seabuoy" and advised them to replace the arrival waypoint in this book with his "more accurate" numbers. Among his hearers were other wannabe explorers who relayed the historic news. In the next month three boats went on the reef right in front of the hotel, the first strandings ever at that place. If you cannot resist "super accurate" waypoints, discard your GPS.

—Use the same datum as the chart, or calibrate each chart as you use it by recording waypoints while positioned at charted features. Note the correction vector on the chart and apply the offset to GPS use (e.g., 0.25 nm NNE).

Never believe claims of accuracy, nor confuse accuracy with precision.

SSB TRANSCEIVER

If sailing in company and leap frogging each other this helps you keep in touch with your friends. It also helps you keep up with the rumor mill which is grinding between the cruisers on your path so you don't feel such a stranger when you arrive. Be careful about weather information received, however, as well as talk of piracy, revolutions, the sky falling in, and so on. Remember this is an entertainment medium. Pure marine SSBs with fixed channels are usually very powerful. The new breed of synthesized digital ham transceivers are less powerful but can be modified to permit marine transmission.

As with all electronics, think of your ampere usage and make sure you can handle it. Some can suck juice like a water maker. In the Caribbean, the radar isn't for fog, it's for confirming landfalls, finding buoys (whenever there are any), and *lordy, lordy,* plying a windward coast so close you can shake hands with the natives. For the singlehander, a well tuned four mile radar with a fence function may help keep watch on crossings.

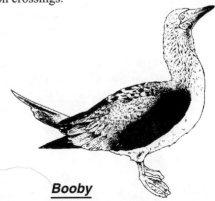

Booby

31

USING THE RADIO

VHF

FM Radio Telephony, or VHF signaling, has reached an interesting stage of development. The rules for using the VHF were developed for poor reception. When Alpha wants to call Bravo, Alpha should say "Bravo, Bravo, Bravo; Alpha, Alpha" and Bravo should reply "Alpha, Bravo; nn", where nn is the number of a working channel to which they both repair. Now that VHF provides high quality reception at a cheap price, every boob has one into which he speaks as would Thomas Alva Edison speak into the ear of Victorola's dog if he had expected the dog to speak back to him.

What's worse, today's Bravo has invented a lottery in which he asks Alpha to "Pick a channel". If he doesn't, then Alpha asks Bravo to do it. Although they call each other several times a day, they will usually pick channels which neither has. This is a noncommittal opening gambit used by VHF lottery players for whom tic-tac-toe is too advanced.

Bridge players will say "six eight" but not press the mike button until the word "eight", thus finessing the other guy into sitting on Channel 8 picking channels with no one. You can always tell a cruiser who plays chess. He will force Alpha to pick a channel first and then say "No, I don't have that, try another" until Alpha hits a good one. Then he talks in HAM codes and International Signals Code over the telephone. These guys also tend to call themselves "THE Bravo", which, incidentally, is against the rules in a few countries and not liked by the Coast Guard unless your transom says "THE Bravo". Guys that say "THIS IS THE Alpha" need severe correction. Guys that say "THIS IS THE SAILING VESSEL Alpha" should have their radios confiscated.

These are the same guys who play CAPCOM MCC (Capsule Communicator, Mission Control Center) and say "Affirma-tive" and "Negative" and "Roger That" 3 times each to a boat two hundred yards away. Deke Slayton took endless ribbing when he slipped up on acknowledging a complex transmission from space with "Roger ... uh ... that". He never repeated it. But today there is a whole new generation of Captain Videos to repeat it and other airwaves eating clichés — endlessly. Myself, I pretend to be Glenn Ford at the controls of his screaming Saberjet calling to his wingman . . .

In most anchorages VHF users are in good hail of each other on low power. Jjust following the normal rules with power down and squelch up will reduce traffic and hasten communications enormously.

The above discussion, as well as the following list of DOs and DON'Ts may be extended to the use of Marine SSB radios as well. *Please* don't clog the calling frequencies as did this actually recorded exchange, edited for brevity as it is.

A: Bravo, Bravo, Bravo. Alpha.

B: Alpha, Alpha, Alpha. Bravo.

A: Bravo, Bravo. Good morning, Ted! Have you got a frequency?

B: Yeah. How about 6-delta? Let's go to 6-delta, 6-delta.

A: No. I haven't got that one programmed. Not programmed. Pick another.

B: Oh. OK. Just a minute. .... How about 6-charlie?

A: Yeah. We can try that. Let's try 6-charlie. What's the frequency?

Here's a list of some DOs rarely DONE.
—turn your power down
—find an idle channel before talking

—talk normally, sideways to the mike

—wait thirty seconds for Bravo to answer

—get off Channel 16 with minimum chat

—use the language your mom taught you

—make each transmission brief

—repeat only if asked

Here are some DON'Ts which are DONE more often than not.

—Don't call yourself anything but your name

—Don't talk HAM or CB, good buddy, QSL.

—Don't eat your microphone

—Don't repeat everything twice

—Don't use channels permanently assigned. (e.g., Coast Guard (21-23), Telephone companies (24-28), or local watersports outfits.

—Don't sit on your handheld's transmit switch, blocking all traffic for hours

—Don't chastise non-English speakers without understanding them

Don't be a Deputy Dawg. That's the guy who sits by his radio and busts in with chapter and verse of the Law of the VHF. He takes up more air time than casual abusers because his dictums are always followed by storms of support from the *Good Citizens* around and Bronx cheers from the *Outlaws and the Rowdies* in the harbor. Unless *Deputy Dawg* is a duly authorized official of the country whose air you are using, you can tell him to take his Barstool Regulations and . . .

CAUTION : never use "buddy channels" to the exclusion of Channel 16.

I recall the two yachts off Montecristi which crossed the steel cables of a 1500 foot tow at night, while the tug's skipper bawled on Channel 16, and I desperately dialed around to find their buddy channel. The hawsers could have sawn the boats in halves, sintering fiberglass and flesh in a heartbeat. It took instead a small bite from a skeg.

EMERGENCY PROCEDURES

VHF Radio Channel 16 is used for all emergency traffic as well as for calling and initial contacts. For this reason, your VHF radio should be left on and monitoring Channel 16 when not in use. There are three levels of ship's safety broadcasts: securitÈ (say-CURE-it-TAYE, French for "safety"), pan (PAHN, Greek for "everywhere") and mayday (MAY-day, kind of French for "help me"). Broadcasts of navigational hazards come after the word SECURIT... said 3 times. For example, a sea mark out or off position, or a barge under tow restricting passage in a channel. Broadcasts of look-outs for personal safety follow the word PAN said 3 times. For example, when the Coast Guard has lost contact with an overdue boat, or when you have lost the ability to maneuver, but life threats don't exit. Broadcasts of imminent danger to life proceed from the word MAYDAY said 3 times. If your boat is sinking, if it's on fire, if someone has been lost overboard, or if there exists any immediate threat to life, do the following:

Ensure the VHF Radio is on Channel 16 Clearly and slowly pronounce the words, "MAYDAY, MAYDAY, MAYDAY".

Say your boat's type and name, "sailing vessel (or trawler) Boatname".

Clearly and slowly give your position, "one mile south of Esperanza on Vieques", or "lattitude 1804, longitude 6528).

State the emergency in simple terms, "we're sinking, sinking", or "man overboard, man overboard"

People handling emergencies at sea often get too busy to stand by the radio. In this case repeat the full MAYDAY several times, hammering on position and type of distress. Force yourself to speak clearly, slowly and with a minimum of words. Everyone understands "man overboard" even with static and intermittent reception. No one can grasp the nature of a rapidly shouted "my husband was looking over the stern and fell in the water and I can't find him".

RADIO TIMES AND FREQUENCIES

Atlantic Std. Time (UTC-4)	Station Call Sign	Freq. 1	Freq. 2	Freq. 3	Freq. 4	Broadcast and Source [see also Listening to the Weather]
530	NMN	4426	6501	8764		NWS Offshore Forecast, Portsmouth
600	WAH	4357	4381	8728	13077	All Forecasts, St.Thomas
	VOA	5980	6165	7405	9590	Voice Of America with news to 0800
630	WVVI	1000				VI Radio Sailor's Report (MTWTF)
635	Arthur	3815	HAM - LSB			West Indian Weather Net Ñ - Barbados
655	WOSO	1030				San Juan weather hourly after news
700	BBC	6195	11865			World News to 0930
	BASRA	4003	EST/EDST			Bahamas Air Sea Rescue weather net
	USB	6215				Antilles Cruisers net (all the way down)
705	4VEH	1030				NWS Offshore Forecasts, from Haiti
710	WVVI	1000				VI Radio Sailor's Report (MTWTF)
	BAR	790				Radio Barbados forecast
745	WWNET	7268	HAM - LSB, EST/EDST			Waterway net US/Bahamas with WX
800	BON	800				Caribbean forecast, Bonaire
	ZNS1	810	1240	1540		Nassau weather
805	ZBVI	780	AM M-F David Jones WX			and ea $\frac{1}{2}$ hr.; 745 Sats.; 945 Sundays
820	USB	4009	Daisy D			Caribbean Safety and Security Net
830	ANT	930				Antigua EC Forecasts (also at 18:25)
	David*	4009				Caribbean weather net with David Jones
845	David*	8104				Caribbean weather net with David Jones
900	WOM	4363	8722	13092	17242	NWS reports (and at 1900), after tfc list
	Maurice	6945	HAM - LSB			French weather net (also 13970 at 1900)
1000	WAH	4357	4381	13077		All Forecasts, St.Thomas
1200	NMN	13089	6501	8764		NWS Offshore Forecast, Portsmouth
1400	WAH	13077				All Forecasts, St.Thomas
1600	BBC	5975	6175	6195	7325	World News every hour to 2400
		9590	9915	11865	15400	
	Herb*	12359				SOUTHBOUND II, VAX498
1800	NMN	13089	8764	6501		NWS Offshore Forecast, Portsmouth
1900	BBC	5975	6165	9915		excellent financial news, again at 2005
	RNI	6020	6165			Netherlands Int'l, good English reporting
2000	VOA	5995	7405	9455	9775	US news with Caribbean report
2200	WAH	4357	4381	8728	13077	All Forecasts, St.Thomas
2330	NMN	4426	6501	8764		NWS Offshore Forecast, Portsmouth

* See chapter, *Listening to the Weather*

Distress &Calling	2182	4125	6215	8291	12290	16420		HAM Hurricane Net is 14325
Alpha	2065	4146	6224	8294	12353	16528	22159	NAVTEX San Juan FEC SITOR WX: 516.8 USB at 0600 then every 4 hours
Bravo	2079	4149	6227	8297	12356	16531	22162	MORSE: Hour FEC: Hour+35
Charlie	2638	4417	6230		12359	16534	22165	NAVTEX Miami FEC SITOR WX: 516.8 USB at 0800 then every 4 hours
Delta	2738	†	6516	‡			22168	Jun-Nov: 4462.5 6344 8534 12992 center freqs.

Expanded Ship to Ship Working Frequencies:

† **4 MHz**: *from* 4000 to 4057 *every 3KHz.*

‡ **8 MHz**: *from* 8101 to 8110, 8116-8122, 8125, 8131-8191 *every 3KHz.*

Other working Frequencies: 18840, 18843   are **18** Alpha, Bravo

22171   is **22** Echo

25115, 25118   are **25** Alpha, Bravo

DIVING IN THE SPANISH VIRGINS

These lovely keys and island pro vide cruising and diving opportu nities as good as or better than their Anglophone cousins to the east, but they have the added spice of "going foreign".

As a diving destination, Puerto Rico is still virgin territory. The Puerto Rico Tourism Company estimates that less than 20 per cent of the snorkeling and scuba opportunities in these islands have been exploited to date. For decades, Puerto Rico has been a Mecca for the sportfising enthusiasts. Tourist dive boat operations are a relatively recent de velopment, and significant charter sail op erations have only begun.

The islands are edged with narrow shelves of white sand beaches by rocky cliffs over coral outcroppings, where snorkleers wan der and wonder. For the scuba divers, most keys and islands are surrounded by precipi tous drop-offs of 12 to 14 fathoms, where the windward walls are brilliantly illumi nated in the morning, and those off the lee ward anchorages are displayed by the after noon sun.

One doesn't have to go to the South Pa cific to explore extensive coral reefs such as the mile-long gormations southeast of Culebrita. The Spanish Virgins are also a submarine photographer's dream.

Lobster season in Puerto Rico, thanks to the crustecean's continous mating season, is year round. Catches are restricted to male adults, or females without eggs, have a cara pace (antennae base to beginning of tail) of 3.5 inches or more.

For the more adventurous, there is La Cor dillera, the 12-mile long string of islets, keys, reefs and sea mounts which stretch from Cayo Icacos, near Cabo San Juan on the mainland, to Arecife Barriles west of Culebra. Many spectacular snorkeling and diving sites here, and elsewhere in the Span ish Virgins, are available from day anchor ages only.

When planning each day's activity, you should cast a cautious eye at the strengths and directions of wind, wave and swell. At many of the recommended day anchorages, and depending on conditions, you should keep an anchor watch aboard while the div ing pary is out. It is of course always best to snorkel or dive upwind and upcurrent of the boat in exposed areas.

DIVE SHOP
DIRECTORY

**PUERTO RICO
DIVER SUPPLY**
Fajardo, Villa Marina
Phone: 863-4300

SEA VENTURES
Puerto del Rey Marina
Phone: 863-Dive

CORAL HEAD DIVERS
Palmas del Mar
Phone: 850-7208

**CULEBRA MARINE
CENTER**
Dewey, canal southside
Phone: 742-3371

CORAL REEF DIVERS
Villa Marina
Phone: 860-REEF

**HUMACAO DIVER
SERVICE CENTER**
Phone: 852-4530

DIVE ISLA CULEBRA
Gene Thomas, Dewey
Phone: 742-3555

**BLUE CARIBE
DIVE CENTER**
Esperanza
Phone: 741-2522

SOLIMAR
(Tank Service)
Esperanza
Phone: 741-8600

NAVIGATING THE SPANISH VIRGINS

Fl 6sec 7M **LA CORDILLERA**

LAS CUCARACHAS

CABO SAN JUAN Fl 15s 26M

"3"

PALOMINOS

ISLETA "1"

CAYO LARGO *(Reef)*

FAJARDO

"6"

PUERTO DEL REY

Fl 4 sec

Fl G 6s

ISLA PIÑEROS

"6"

ROOSEVELT ROADS *(NAVY BASE)*

"8"

"9" "10" "7"

"9"

PUNTA ARENAS *(Green Beach)*

VIEQUES

POINT LIMA

CAYO SANTIAGO

HUMACAO

CAYO BATATA

N

PALMAS DEL MAR Q Fl 3M

PUERTO YABUCOA *(Refinery)*

Fl R 4sec

Fl G 3sec

EAST COAST of PUERTO RICO

POINT YEGUAS

POINT TUNA Gp Fl (2) 30sec 25M

The Spanish Virgin Islands embrace 400 square miles to the west of the U.S. Virgin Islands. Unlike the USVIs, Puerto Rico has an extensively developed industrial and agricultural infrastructure. But like the USVI, the Spanish Virgins are entirely dependent on tourism, yet they are many years behind in the development of tourism infrastructure. Bad for the typical resort tourist, good for the cruiser. It means unaffected townspeople, undisturbed anchorages, pristine beaches and productive fishing (with a year-round lobster season). Ashore, the Spanish Virgins offer immersion in the Spanish Caribbean with the escape clause of bilingualism and the convenience of U.S. institutions. There are three cruising areas in the Spanish Virgins: La Cordillera, Culebra and Vieques. Be sure to schedule ample time to enjoy each. Review Sailing Directions for Vieques Sound.

December through March, distant gales often create swell in exposed northern anchorages, and some day anchorages might be untenable. Fortunately, the lovely harbors of the south coast of Vieques and the reef anchorages of Culebra, Icacos and Palominos are unaffected. Cold fronts that make it this far south are often stalled or have dissipated into troughs which persist for several days. While not good for the avid sailor, these conditions make for fluky winds which in turn create diving and snorkeling opportunities across La Cordillera, in Culebra's outlying keys, and on Vieques' north coast.

USING GPS

GPS WAYPOINTS

All GPS coordinates in this guide are given to the nearest tenth of a mile. This should satisfy either WGS-84 (NAD83) and WGS-72 datum. These waypoints were taken on site and confirmed several times each on different occasions. All bearings given have intentionally been made as simple and mnemonic as possible, given the marks they refer to. Every attempt was made to make GPS waypoints with safe searoom, and which coincide with critical compass bearings.

NOTATION

The format used is always **DDMM** (Degrees, Minutes), eliminating the folderol and fritter of ° and ' signs, and N and W designations for Latitude and Longitude. For example, I write **2845** instead of **28° 45' N**. Since the area covered by this book is 15-26°N latitude and 60-80°W longitude, there shouldn't be any confusion with this simpler notation. However, if you do get it twisted up, you will no doubt recover your error since 28°45'W is the longitude of Faial, in the Azores, and you probably don't want that right now. In any case, there shall surely be the normal complement of cruisers in Georgetown to rail against the notation. They're usually the ones who don't read the book fore-to-aft, and therefore they miss the keys to its interpretations.

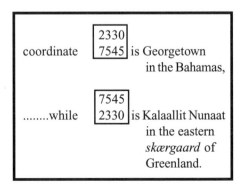

STRATEGIES FOR PASSAGE MAKING

The greatest underestimation we cruisers make is upon the stamina of the crew. We often make judgments based on our younger selves. There is hardly a sailing leg that can't be shortened by 10-to -30 percent in time, and 20-to-60 percent in adrenaline, by one simple practice: start early and arive early.

LET LANDFALL DETERMINE DEPARTURE

Plan your departure in time to make landfall in favorable light, arriving with <u>several hours</u> of daylight left. The Spanish Virgins are full of anchorages where you will need the sun high and over your shoulder for the

Get away from the crowd. Get near the sea. Get your dinghy up. Go to one shallow hook. Go to a departure anchorage the day before. Clean up all your rodes. Make sea-ready on deck and below. Take in a reef while at anchor. It will be easier to shake out than to tie in later. Take a swim and a snorkel. Eat a candlelight dinner, listen to music, read a book. Turn in early. Turn out an hour before anchors-up. Watch the dawn, or listen to the night. Hoist a cup of coffee or two. Then hoist sail, hoist that shallow single rode, fall back on the wind, and slide out. You shall be up on the first leg by an hour or more, sometimes much more. And you have an added bonus of a shortened first leg. It sure beats doing all that work just before sailing out with muddy decks and sweaty crew.

first time you enter. A 3 p.m. landfall may dictate a 7 a.m. start. If you've been accustomed to waking at 9 a.m. and having your Wheaties before addressing the world, and you are reluctant to break that custom, you may be in trouble.

Have a variety of departure plans ready for different breaks in the weather and for different landfalls.

—Plot several routes contingent on breaking weather.

—Depart at the earliest time called for by your contingent routes so that you can make changes underway in response to changes in the weather.

—Every delay in departure creates a risk upon arrival.

—Reckon on 20 percent less speed to windward than you are accustomed to. If you get more, great!

CONTINGENCY PLANNING

Leave yourself enough time. Most of us are fairly adequate when planning contingencies along the route. The discussion above illustrates contingencies of actual landfalls. When most cruisers quote how long it took them to make a passage they usually talk about offing to offing, ignoring the time taken with departures and arrivals. I quote hours of passage making from ready to up anchor to anchors down and set. When planning your route, add in contingencies for getting underway and getting settled shown below.

Contingencies Getting Underway...

—the over-the-shoulder light needed to wend your way out of a reef anchorage,

—the anchors-up drills with lots of mangrove mud to clean off oneself and the boat,

—getting the dinghy and motor aboard.

One wonders sometimes how one ever escapes some harbors. On the landfall side are other factors.

Contingencies of Landfall...

—there may be reefs to navigate in over-the-shoulder light,

—time to select a safe and shallow spot in which to anchor,

—getting the dinghy and motor down before shoreside closings,

—the office hours at the customs shack for clearing in,

—properly put the boat to bed in a new anchorage with an eye to 2 a.m. anchor drills.

Tally the hours for the above lists, then add a couple of hours of safety margin to ensure you get in well before dark.

PUERTO RICO'S EAST COAST

The Spanish Virgin's western boundary is home to six major marinas and five haul out yards. In the shelter of Puerto Rico's highest peak and America's only tropical rain forest, this coast hosts offshore a wealth of cruise-worthy islands.

Yolas*, or *Piñeros

Blue Marlin

PALMAS DEL MAR

Enter in good water directly from the east. The anchorage may be temporarily used, some guides notwithstanding. There is good holding in 10-12 feet everywhere except the northeast corner which has silted to a depth of 5-6 feet near the seawall, but that's where you want to be to avoid rolling in swell which can sometimes penetrate the harbor.

Palmas is a resort and condominium project along the lines of Puerto Cervo in Sardinia and José Banús in Spain. Golf, tennis, scuba, sport fishing and sail charters are available to owners or guests of the hotel, marina or shipyard. At a condo slip,

in the marina, or laid up ashore at the yard, this harbor affords reasonable hurricane protection. Boats fared well here as hurricane Hugo passed by. If you lay up ashore, ensure for yourself that the jackstands are lashed securely together with nylon warp, and using Spanish windlasses to maintain tension. During Hugo, boats on the hard blew over due to inadequate lashings.

Chez Daniel is an excellent authentic French restaurant. A fisherman's restaurant and seafood store is in the southeast corner of the anchoring basin.

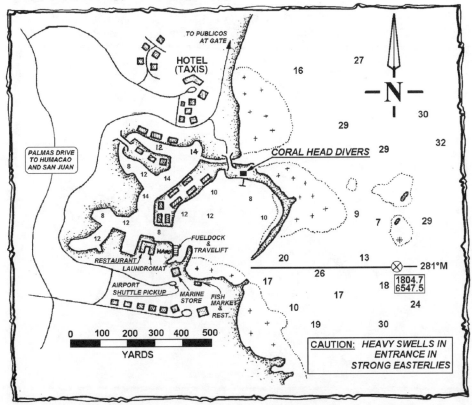

CAYO SANTIAGO

Also called "Monkey Island", Cayo Santiago is a free range for the Caribbean Primate Research Center. It is inhabited by well over 1000 monkeys, whose crazy antics include biting persistent tourists. Best to stay on the sand beach and enjoy the cerulean water and the abundant snorkeling behind the island. It is not permitted to go ashore other than on the beach. Do not molest nor feed the monkeys. Enter from the south and east.

Day charterers and snorkelers from Palmas del Mar may join you, but this anchorage is normally deserted late afternoons and nights.

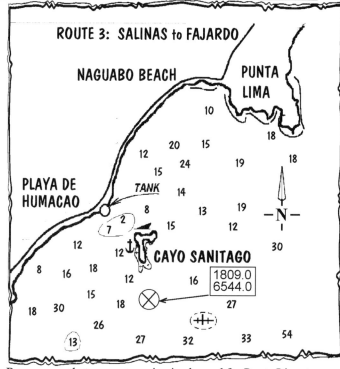

Rumors are that a resort marina is planned for Punta Lima to the north to compete with Puerto del Rey and Palmas del Mar.

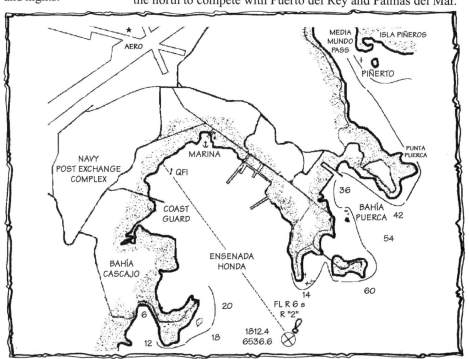

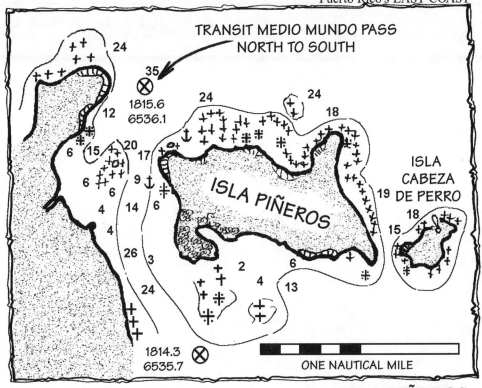

TRANSIT MEDIO MUNDO PASS
NORTH TO SOUTH

1815.6
6536.1

ISLA PIÑEROS

ISLA
CABEZA
DE PERRO

1814.3
6535.7

ONE NAUTICAL MILE

ISLA PIÑEROS

A well protected anchorage which is quite secluded during the week, yet it is only 3 miles south of the largest marina in the Caribbean. This island is part of the Roosevelt Roads Navy Base and the Navy does not allow going ashore. Nonetheless one can anchor overnight for excellent swimming and snorkeling. The cove in the northern reef is a nice lunch anchorage in summer months when the wind is south of east. Enter Pasaje Medio Mundo from the north where the rocks west of the pass are clearly visible. The shoal on the island's southwest corner extends quite far and is less visible. It is not recommended to pass between Isla Piñeros and Cabeza de Perro. Call Puerto del Rey's harbormaster at 860-1000 or on VHF Channel 71 for information regarding Navy maneuvers.

ROOSEVELT ROADS NAVAL STATION

An emergency refuge for all but retired career military and their guests, Roosevelt Roads has a small marina with marine store, limited dockage, med-moorings at the seawall and some moorings. The marina stands by on VHF Ch.16. Telephone (787) 865-3297.

Turn to the chapter about Navy Range Vieques for more on the mission of Roosevelt Roads and how it affects, and helps, the cruising community.

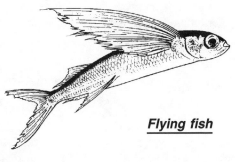

Flying fish

43

PUERTO DEL REY

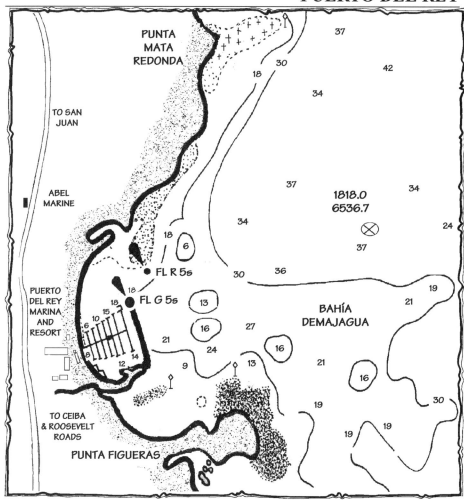

If visiting San Juan or picking up crew, Puerto del Rey is the port of convenience. With 750 slips and long term land storage it is the largest and most modern marina in the Caribbean. Atlantic Canvas and Sails is here as well as any yacht service desired. Puerto del Rey's 80-ton Travelift is avail- able for emergencies seven days a week, 24 hours a day. Call the harbormaster on VHF channel 71 or 16 for a slip or a transient dock, or anchor temporarily in the turning basin inside the breakwater north of the docks. A rental car agency is on site.

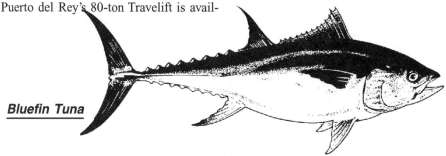

Bluefin Tuna

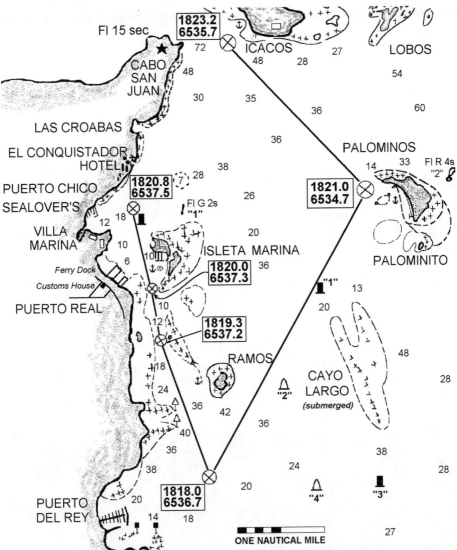

The district of Fajardo caters to yachting enthusiasts from around the world. Major sailing events such as the Heineken International Cup and CORT regattas, as well as the Club Nautico de Puerto Rico's Round Puerto Rico Race are hosted from Fajardo.

Fajardo lies at the foot of the only tropical rain forest in US jurisdiction, the 28,000 acre El Yunque national forest, where annually 100 billion gallons of rain nurture 240 species of trees. The forest's 3,532 foot peak, El Toro, is visible throughout the Spanish Virgins. Excepting Chez Daniel in Palmas del Mar, Restaurant du Port at Puerto del Rey and Rosas seafood restaurant in Puerto Real, sailors ashore seeking fine dining need a car.

Ports on the mainland can be approached via the ship channel or via the "inside route", behind the keys and the reefs using a careful eyeball method. If taking the inside route, watch for a cross set at the GPS waypoint shown on the chartlet just south of Isleta.

When approaching downwind from the east, be careful to avoid Cayo Largo. The ground swells to windward of this dangerous reef are not always visible from their backs.

Ramos is a private island. You may anchor outside the string of floats off the beach with which the owner has marked his territory, but you may not go ashore.

ISLETA

Anchor at Isleta west of the marked shoal in the bight of the two islands; close to the marina you will suffer from the ferry wakes. There are two ferry services to Puerto Real, one for residents of the condominium and marina, the other for visitors at a cost. The ferries run from 6:30 to 21:30, quarter after and quarter of the hour.

PUETO REAL

Except for dredged ferry channels, Puerto Real is shoal and windward. It is best approached by dinghy or by the ferries from Isleta Marina. Ferries to and from Culebra

and Vieques can be had here. Some provisions are at Big Johns across from the Isleta ferry dock. Dine at Rosas Seafood, a short walk inland from there.

VILLA MARINA

Villa Marina, with 250 slips and a 60 ton Travelift, caters mostly to power craft. Marine stores Skipper Shop and El Pescador behind Villa Marina are the most extensively stocked in the area. On the same street are Fajardo Canvas and Sails, and Re-Power Marine Services for engine, prop and machine shop needs.

PUERTOCHICO/SEA LOVERS

Immediately northeast of Villa Marina are the marinas of Sea Lovers, near the beach, and Puerto Chico, larger and to the east behind the seawall. Puerto Chico has a fuel dock and handles drafts to seven feet. Sea Lovers is for smaller craft.

LAS CROABAS

Las Croabas is a cheap and fun place to haul with lots of nearby tipico restaurants and bars. There are no hardware stores nearby.

ISLA PALOMINOS

A jewel of a tropical island from which to watch the sun set over El Yunque on a last night's return to Fajardo. If headed east, Palominos is a must to break up what can be a bear of a windward close-hauled leg.

Facilities ashore are leased by El Conquistador resort on the mainland. Anchor between the harbor's central shoal and the island, or close to Palominitos, to avoid the wash of the hotel ferries.

Whether running west from the USVIs, or beating eastward on the start of a cruise, Palominos is a fine farewell or introduction to the Spanish Virgins.

Having overnighted in Palominos, take a morning sail down to Isabel Segunda for lunch and a look at the fort. To continue on to Culebra, tack up to Diablo from behind Palominos, continue tacking east along the Cordillera, making successively shorter tacks as you gain lee from Culebra. Let anchors-down at Luis Peña. (See sketch).

14   **33**

30

1821.0
6534.7

⊗   24

DIVE **40**
MOORINGS   O + ⌁ ⊥

28   **25**   **5**   **10**

FL R 4s

5

ISLA
PALOMINOS

5   **1**

⊥   O

1

2

ONE NAUTICAL MILE

PALOMINITOS

Fisherman's Homecoming

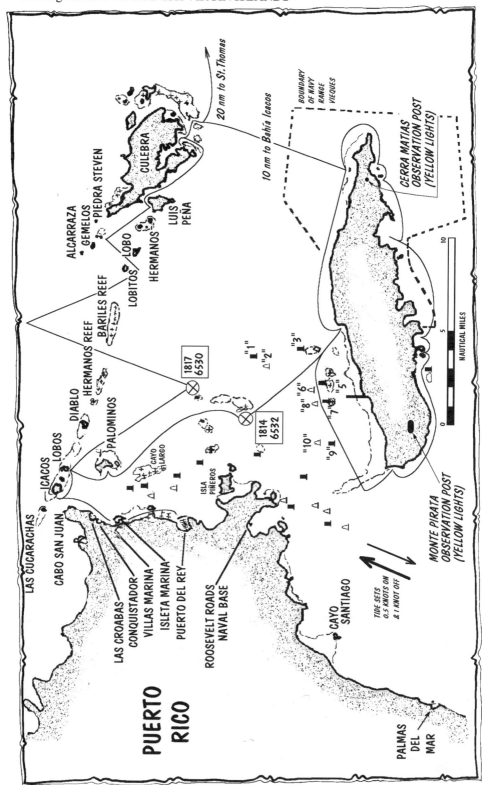

SAILING DIRECTIONS, VIEQUES SOUND

From **Vieques Sound** (pronounced vee-AYE-case) until the end of the British Virgin Islands, the islands are within sight of each other. Nonetheless, you should not try to cross this stretch in one bound.

For many years I have experimented with sailing to windward across Vieques Sound. I find that I save a couple of hours by tacking in the area south of the **Cordillera**, where the current and chop is less adverse, into the lee of **Culebra**. However, a strong motorsailor can barrel down the middle in heavy chop and contrary current with more stress in less time. The south coast of Vieques can be tough going to windward in onshore easterlies against the equatorial current. It's best to sail the south coast of Vieques downwind and with several stops at its beautiful beaches and anchorages. In short, if you circumnavigate the Spanish Virgins, do so clockwise.

Cross the shoaly Sound with pleasantly short and easy trips. Notice from the chart that to avoid a visit to **Isla Palominos**, one would have to go out of one's way and bash nine-12 hours to windward across Vieques Sound. From Palominos one can use the lee of Culebra and the keys west of it to pleasantly sneak-tack one's way to Dewey in only six to eight hours.

CURRENTS AND TIDES

Cruisers in the Spanish Virgins should take special note of set in Vieques Sound. Yachties from the Virgins on their first trek to Puerto Rico and back are surprised to find it sometimes takes twice the time to sail east as it took to sail west, something to bear in mind when setting out late in the day from Fajardo. You don't want to be caught out among the reefs in bad light! The Equatorial Current flows west northwest in this area at a clip of 0.4 to 0.7 knots. When it mounts the shallow plateau of the Sound, sheering forces increase its velocity in chaotic ways. The tide floods west and ebbs east, but on the Sound's north and south borders tidal flow is more north-south as it pours onto or spills off the Sound's shallow plateau. These currents approach 1 knot on flood, a half-knot on ebb. While these effects are not extreme, when taken together, they can lead to unpredictable landfalls and arrival times. Since you want to arrive at reef entrances in favorable light, conservative course planning is essential.

The shallow Sound can whip up a vicious chop above 15 knots, impeding windward progress. If motor- sailing, sheet in hard and tack the chop in comfort. With sail up, you'll make better time over ground as well.

STAGING

Start at Punta Arenas and take whatever route you wish to get to Culebra, just not direct. Stop first at Roosevelt Roads for retired militaries, the Fajardo boat yards for those not hauling in Palmas del Mar, or Isla Palominos for those wanting to scrub their bottoms and enjoy a Bahamas-like respite before going eastward over the Sound.

A stop at Culebra, is required before pressing on to the hurly burly of the commercial U.S. Virgins. Anchor at the little beach behind Luis Peña. Carry on to Dewey or Ensenada Honda next day. Culebra is also a place to wait out summer storms. Some cruisers make a pattern of summer in Culebra, winter in the Virgins, never moving their yachts more than a few miles in an east or west direction all year. They put down a hurricane mooring in a select spot before the seasonal rush begins and summer there in security, watching the fire drills when the exodus from the Virgins begins with each hurricane warning.

Wait favorable conditions in Dakity Harbor or Bahía Almodûvar before moving on to St.Thomas or Puerto Rico. If bound for a circumnavigation of Vieques, set sail from there for Bahía del Sur after a ensuring a cold Navy test range.

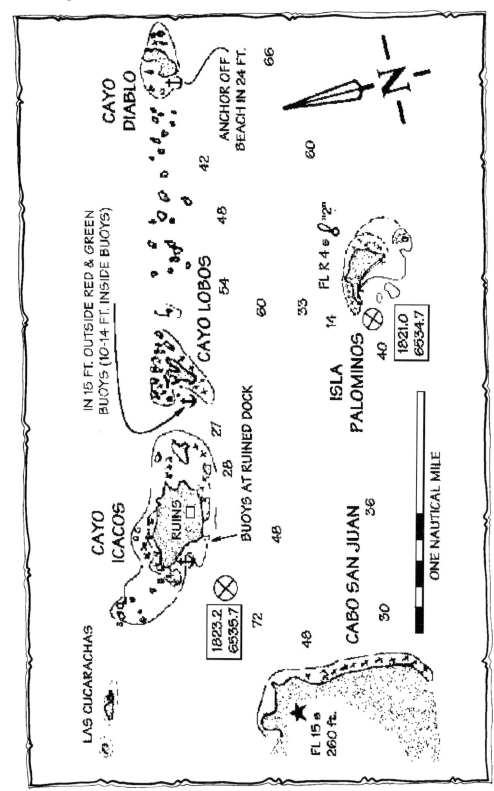

LA CORDILLERA

This 12-mile chain of islets and reefs is Puerto Rico's East Coast Marine Reserve. The larger keys can be used to day-anchor the mother boat in the lee of the easterly trades and in shelter of northerly swell in the winter.

Diving expeditions can then be run by dingy to the surrounding reefs and walls. Diving opportunities on the Cordillera are constrained in the winter months by wind and swell. Northerly swell and anything but mild easterlies are unusual in the summer months. In general, look for minimum swell days with a favorable wind of 15 knots or less before choosing your day anchorage and dive sites.

CAYO ICACOS

Arrive at the waypoint shown on the chart and then proceed into the cove of deeper water by eyeball, snuggling up to the white sand beach in seven feet of glass clear water. Under prevailing trades this can be a good night anchorage and provides endless diving, snorkeling and shelling on the surrounding reefs and secluded beaches. It might be a little rolly in winter, however.

CAYO LOBOS

This is a privately owned resort island with a protected harbor marked by red and green floats. Make a day anchorage just inside or outside the buoys and well off the channel, respecting the access and privacy of the owners.

CAYO DIABLO

Shoal draft vessels can work close in to the beach, while deeper drafts must avoid the coral formations and anchor in three-to-four fathoms of clear sand farther out.

The rocks and islets downwind can be dived with a reliable motorized tender. Be sure there is enough anchor rode and that it includes chain. This is a day anchorage only, and only in settled conditions of less than 15 knots east.

There is a diveboat mooring on the east shore.

LOS HERMANOS AND BARRILES

To the east of Cayo Diablo are two long reefs called Hermanos and Barriles which, though in open sea, can provide quite productive diving during calm conditions. These reefs and the many islets strung out to the east, which belong to the Culebra group, are for experienced divers.

The Cordilleras, a snorkler's and diver's paradise

CULEBRA AND ITS OUT ISLANDS

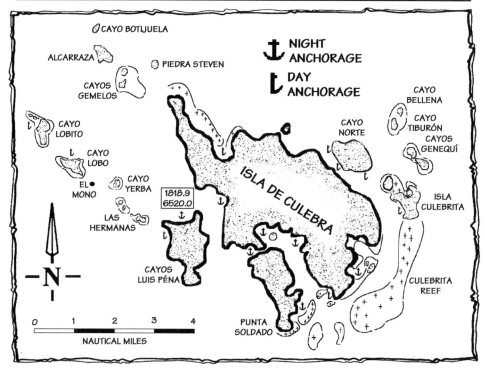

Unspoiled Isla de Culebra is a winter retreat for some and a permanent expatriate refuge for others. Most people are attracted by its seclusion, its spectacular beaches and the quaint and insular town of Dewey.

Unexploited diving opportunities abound in the rocks, islets and full boarded islands centered on Culebra. Dive any number of day anchorages, though swell can affect them in the winter months. Culebra and its outlying islands can absorb the serious cruiser or diver for weeks. Arriving from Puerto Rico, make your landfall at Luis Peña. Arriving from the Virgin Islands or overseas, anchor overnight at Dakity Harbor behind the reef entrance to Ensenada Honda. Proceed next morning to the top of Ensenada Honda to clear in at Dewey.

CAYOS LOBO AND LOBITO

Unless you have a large launch, these keys are too far downwind to safely visit by dinghy from Luis Peña. However, under settled east southeasterlies with no north-

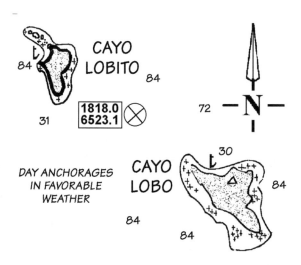

DAY ANCHORAGES
IN FAVORABLE
WEATHER

ern swell, it is possible to use day anchorages at either key. There are both reefs and walls to satisfy snorkelers and scuba buffs. As with most day anchorages, the skipper might want to post an anchor watch aboard while the diving party is out. Dive up wind and current of the dinghy.

CAYO LUIS PEÑA

In settled easterlies, the beach on the north shore of Luis Peña provides anchoring in clear white sand roads between patches of coral rock. Stay in one-to-two fathoms, since the water shoals quickly. The anchorage inside the reef is available to drafts of five feet and less. In winter the northwestern point of Culebra shields the anchorage from the worst of the northeast swell. Luis Peña is an uninhabited wildlife refuge with hiking paths and secluded beaches. Except on weekends, you are likely to be alone here, where you will toast the sun disappearing spectacularly over the rocky skerries of Las Hermanas, backed by the majestic peaks of the El Yunque rain forest.

In light conditions, this is a great place from which to launch diving expeditions in gofast dinghies. To the north are the reefs of Culebra's Punta del Noroeste and the offshore keys of Alcarraza, Los Gemelos and Piedra Steven. Closer yet to the west are Las Hermanas rocks and Cayo Yerba.

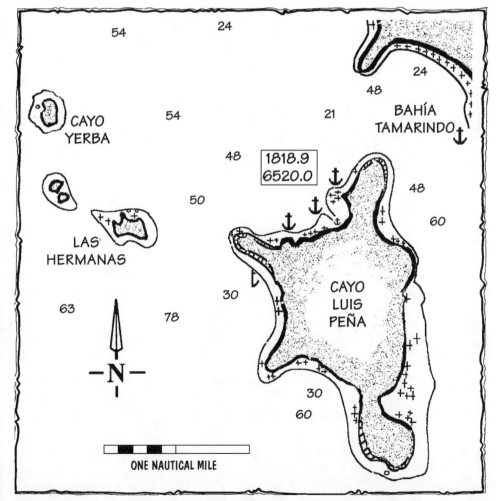

CULEBRA

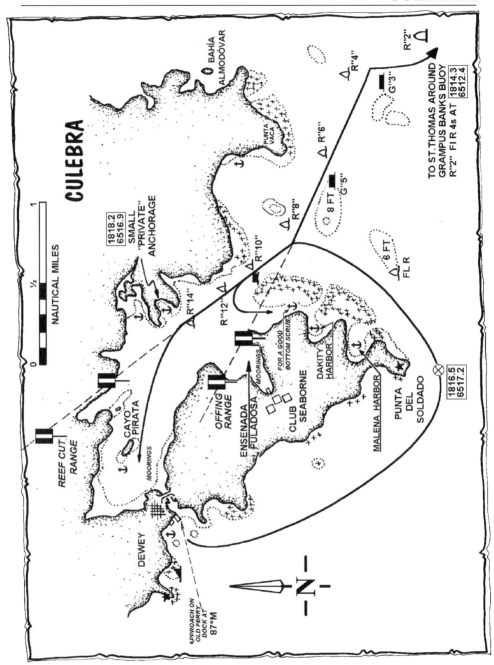

CULEBRA NATIONAL WILDLIFE REFUGE

Large seabird colonies are protected by this sea park which consists of 23 keys and islands and four large tracts of land on Culebra itself. Luis Peña and Culebrita are open for exploration ashore from sunrise to sunset.

ENSENADA HONDA

The narrow reef entrance is clearly marked by green can No. 9 and red buoy No. 10. Enter between the buoys. The holding is poor right off the town. The boats there look like they are at anchor but most are on moorings. To be near town, anchor in 16 feet on a bottom of sand and mud west of Cayo Pirata. The finest anchorage to be had within Ensenada Honda is behind the reef at Dakity Harbor in two-to-three fathoms over white sand. Malena Harbor to the southwest can be tricky; it is best left to local powerboats. Dinghy to the happy hour at the Club Seabourne pool at the foot of Fulladosa Bay.

FLAMENCO BEACH

This is a spectacularly beautiful beach whose anchorage is untenable in northerly wind or swell which often occurs in the winter months. Under those conditions you can visit by road with your camera. It's over the hill from the airport. Under favorable conditions it is a great sand anchorage until ebb tide when you might find it starts to roll. Plan your trip to go in for lunch on a rise of tide and exit on the ebb in the afternoon. You won't regret it.

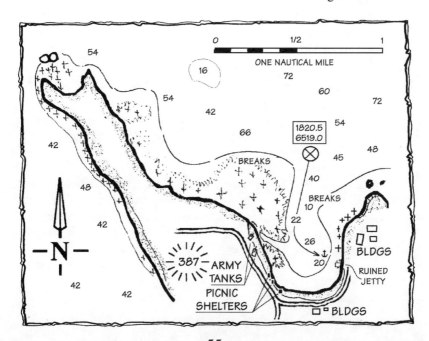

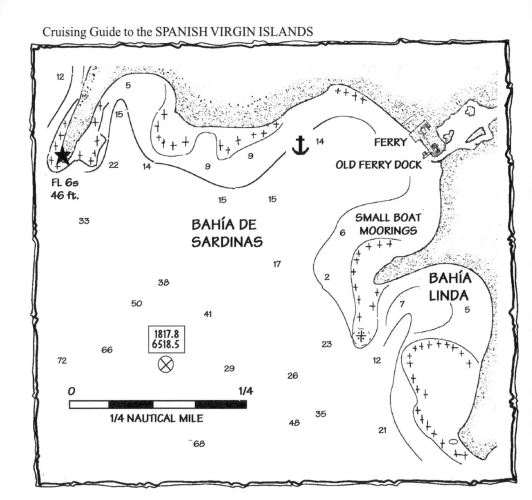

BAHÍA SARDINAS

Dewey can be entered at night by Bahía Sardinas. Position yourself one half mile south of the flashing seven second light marking the reefs west and north of the harbor entrance. From there take up a heading of 87° Magnetic on the brightly lit old ferry dock on the south edge of town. Anchor in 12 feet of clear water over white sand to the northwest of the new ferry dock. The ferries stop running after 6 p.m., so your night should be a comfortable one. You shall be conveniently waked by the 7 a.m. ferry, however, should you oversleep. The above

advice notwithstanding, it is not advisable to be sailing these waters at night.

If coming from the east you shall need to clear customs and immigration in Dewey from the Ensenada Honda side. Customs is at the airport, a five minute walk from El Batey restaurant whose dinghy dock is a long ell pier northwest of the anchorage, just north of the high school stadium which is visible from the water. See the chartlet of Ensenada Honda.

El Batey has the best sandwiches on the island.

Map of Dewey

TO AIRPORT & EL BATEY

ENSENADA HONDA

⚓

BUENA VISTA

SALISBURY

MKT.

HDWE. MKT.

MKT.

ROMERO

TOWN DOCK

HOSPITAL

MARQUEZ

LA LOMA→

CASTELAR

ESCUDA

BRIDGE

THE DINGHY DOCK REST.

POST OFFICE

DRAW

CULEBRA CONNECTIONS

TOURISM OFFICE

PARADISE

BANK

FACTORY

LAUNDRY

FUEL

BAKERY

FIRE STATION

FERRY

MARTA'S

OLD FERRY DOCK

FISH STORE

CULEBRA MARINE CENTER

BAHIA DE SARDINAS

-N-

DEWEY

See Bruce and Kathy at La Loma art shop, above the town dock, for the latest skinny on what's happening in Culebra. The town offers a variety of restaurants, bars and boutiques with conveniently staggered, if not randomly chosen, opening hours.

Ferries to Fajardo run frequently from Dewey, if you bypassed Fajardo but want to visit it from Culebra. Fresh vegetables are available by truck from the mainland twice a week. The truck parks in front of the Post Office.

TURTLE WATCH PROGRAM

Playa Resaca and Playa Brav on the north coast of Culebra, east of Flamenco Beach are turtle nesting beaches. The Culebra Leatherback Project conducts nightly beach surveys from April 1 to August 30th. Interested cruisers may participate l previous arrangement with projec agement. To participate, call 809-742-0115.

BAHÍA DE ALMODÓVAR

Bahía de Almodóvar and Dakity Harbor are the most tranquil anchorages of Culebra. Round Culebra at Punta Vaca into Canal del Sur. Enter Puerto Manglar heading 325°M on a large wedding cake of a house overlooking the bay. Pass between small red and green markers in three fathoms. Round the double mangrove islet of Pelaita through a 10-foot deep channel and between another set of markers. You are now in Bahía Almodóvar's deep, still waters. Anchor west of the reef in two-to-four fathoms of white sand and gin clear water. The cooling trades blow over the reef out of a clear horizon, where the lights of St. Thomas come on at night. This harbor is locally called La Pelá or Manglar.

ISLA CULEBRITA

Within the northern arms of Culebrita is a 400 yard diameter basin with 7 to 25 feet of clear water bordered by white beaches. If you missed Flamenco, be sure to do Culebrita. Hike to the seaward pools known locally as "the Jacuzzis". Snorkel the nearby reefs and ledges, or dive the Cayos Ballena, Tiburón and Geniqu' a mile to the north. In 20 knots of wind or more there can be heavy seas between Cayos Geniquì and Culebrita. Once inside, easterly seas disappear, but occasional heavy northerly swell may penetrate the bay in winter. Overnight here only in settled weather with no north swell forecast.

If conditions don't permit a visit to the northern anchorage, stop on the southwest coast of Culebrita. Visit the northern beach afoot by mounting the hill to the old lighthouse. Take a camera. Anchor by the small piers north of Punta Arenisca in 16 feet of sand surrounded by 4 to 6 foot coral heads and to the east of a 72 foot drop-off for snorkeling and diving. Culebrita Reef stretches almost two miles from here to the south southwest. For serious fishing expeditions, Grampus

CAYO NORTE

Depending on swell, two-day anchorages are available on the southwest shore for diving expeditions by dinghy. Anchor on the shelf in 25 feet of sand off rocky ledges with a 72-foot wall to the west. In settled light easterlies such as in the summer months, one can anchor overnight on the east end of the southern shore in 18 feet of sand, west southwest of the red fisherman's cottage, sheltered by the breaking reef to the east.

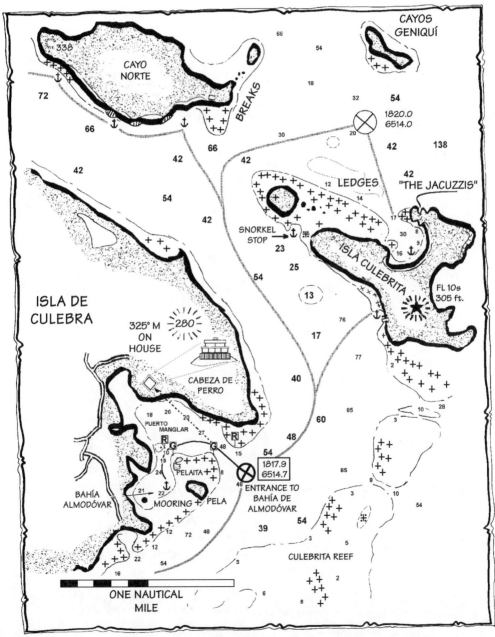

CAYOS GENIQUÍ

CAYO NORTE

338

72

66

66

42

42

66

BREAKS

54

66

18

32

54

1820.0
6514.0

20

30

42

138

42

42

42

54

12

LEDGES

14

"THE JACUZZIS"

42

17

ISLA DE CULEBRA

42

54

SNORKEL STOP

23

25

54

13

30

16

9

ISLA CULEBRITA

FL 10s
305 ft.

325° M
ON HOUSE

280

CABEZA DE PERRO

76

17

77

40

60

85

2

10

28

3

18

26

PUERTO MANGLAR

20

27

R

G

G

48

15

R

48

54

1817.9
6514.7

ENTRANCE TO
BAHÍA DE ALMODÓVAR

85

8

10

10

19

24

PELAITA

8

BAHÍA ALMODÓVAR

21

22

MOORING

PELA

48

39

54

12

72

48

3

5

54

12

22

54

16

3

6

CULEBRITA REEF

2

8

ONE NAUTICAL MILE

59

VIEQUES, NAVY RANGE

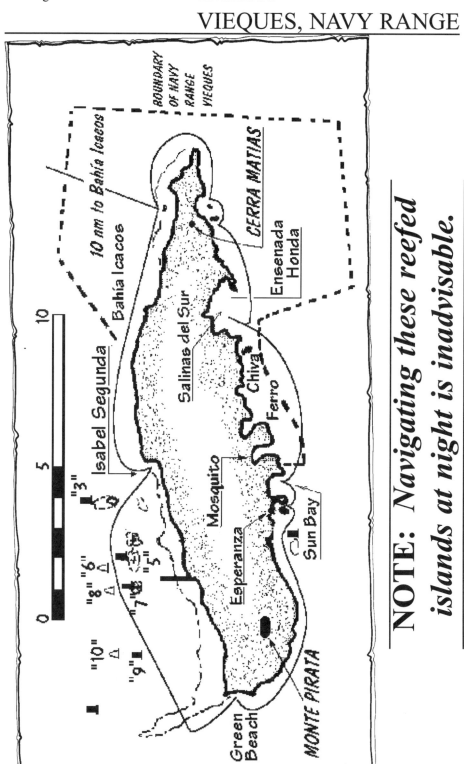

NOTE: *Navigating these reefed islands at night is inadvisable.*

Many consider these anchorages and beaches the best of all Virgin Island anchorages. They have been left untouched by developers. They have been off limits most of this century, and they have been little used as anchorages since they were formed.

For most of the 20th century the US Navy has used much of Culebra and Vieques for weapons training. US and NATO navies still use the east end of Vieques for land, air and sea based war games. However, the anchorages and beaches are available for use by yachts when the test range is not hot, as they say.

Weekends are *normally* available, but these anchorages may be visited at any time with Navy permission, which is easy to get. Call VIEQUES RANGE CONTROL on VHF channel 16 and inquire if the range is *hot*. If no response after repeated tries within VHF range of the observation posts on Cerro Matías (see chartlet for Salinas de Sur) or Monte Pirata on the island's west end, consider the range available for your use. If,

after diligent but fruitless attempts to contact the Navy, you wander into a closed zone, not to worry, the Navy will graciously let you know in good time. Keep VHF channel 16 on.

It is unrealistic to depend on constant harmony between the Navy's use of its test range, your cruising schedule and your draw of wind and wave on that coast. A good plan is to launch a cruise of Vieques from Culebra. While enjoying superb *culebrense* cruising, you can watch for a window of favorable weather and no operations in the Vieques Navy ranges. When that happens, which it shall, you'll be off for a memorable cruise.

When visiting the beaches, do not go inshore. Do not molest any devices found on the beach — certainly not shells made by man! As a service to the yachting community, Puerto del Rey Marina in Fajardo will provide the Navy's weekly Vieques hot exercise schedule. Call Puerto del Rey HARBORMASTER on VHF 16 or 71, or dial 860-1000 by land line.

Harbor at Isabel II looking southwest

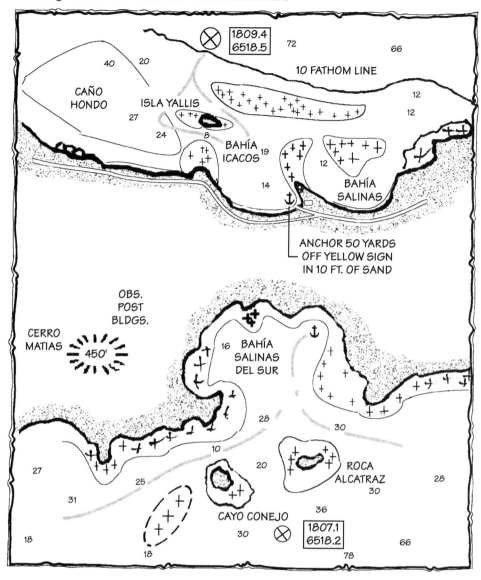

BAHÍA ICACOS

Bahía Icacos is a beautifully protected azure bay surrounded by ranks of reefs for both protection and snorkeling. Approach from the west with high afternoon light over your shoulder. The narrow gap between the mainland shoals and Isla Yallis has eight feet of water and is sheltered from swell. Because there is no clear sand road in this channel, it may be comfortable for only shallow draft vessels. Deeper drafts may take the 17-foot minimum depth of the channel between the breakers on the seaward reef and Isla Yallis. Bahía Salinas, to the east, is a secluded beach exposed to northerly swells through a gap in the reefs. Leave the bay the way you entered by Isla Yallis, in the morning and with light over your shoulder.

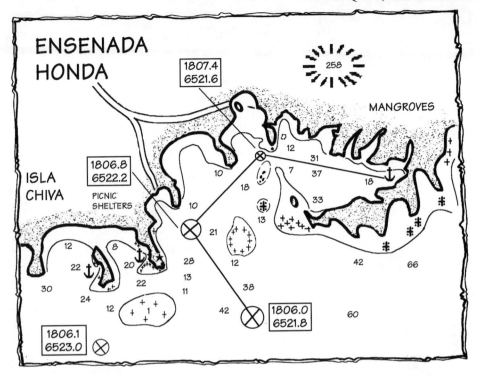

SALINAS DEL SUR

Under east to north winds this is a calm, beach lined anchorage. Tuck up into the northeast corner behind the reef and select a patch of bare sand to anchor in 10 feet of water. If you use the beach, don't go further inland nor pick up man-made objects.

BAHÍA CHIVA

Bahía Chiva is a US Navy beach area with many picnic shelters, the anchorage can nonetheless be quiet and private. Holding is good in fern and fan covered sand. The calmest anchorage is in 10 feet of water in front of the southernmost picnic shelter, close to the beach and covered from swell by the reef west of the point. On the west side of Isla Chiva is a fine anchorage tight up against its northern end, or, for a lunch stop with snorkeling, off the rock crevice at the island's midpoint.

ENSENADA HONDA

Ensenada Honda is a wonderfully tranquil and secluded mangrove anchorage and a fine hurricane hole for hurricanes that cooperate and don't blow from the west. Enter northwest by north on the first point of land inside the bay. Turn northeast at three fathoms toward a baby mangrove off the tip of the third point. When north of a set of rocks called Los Galafatos ("The Thieves"), turn east southeast for the anchorage. See the chartlet for waypoints

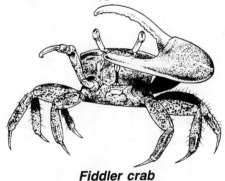

Fiddler crab

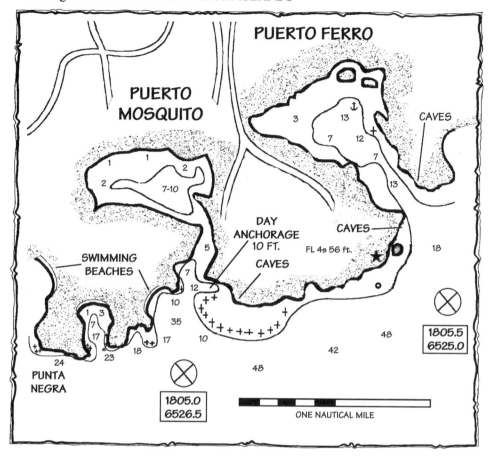

BIOLUMINESCENT BAYS OF VIEQUES

Both Puerto Ferro and Puerto Mosquito are strongly phosphorescent. If you don't overnight at them, you can visit by dinghy from Sun Bay or Esperanza, or you can take night tours from Esperanza arranged through several local dive and tour operators.

PUERTO FERRO

Puerto Ferro is a mangrove anchorage with a narrow entrance and only a seven foot controlling depth on the bar. A day anchorage is feasible outside the bar when the wind is north of east or less than 15 knots south of east.

PUERTO MOSQUITO

Puerto Mosquito is accessible only to drafts under five feet, or slightly more at high tide (with infinite patience). A day anchorage is available which, under settled conditions, can be used for snorkel trips to the rocks and caves about the harbor's mouth. To the west of the entrance is perhaps the loveliest palm lined, white sand, azure water swimming beach in the Caribbean.

CIVIL VIEQUES

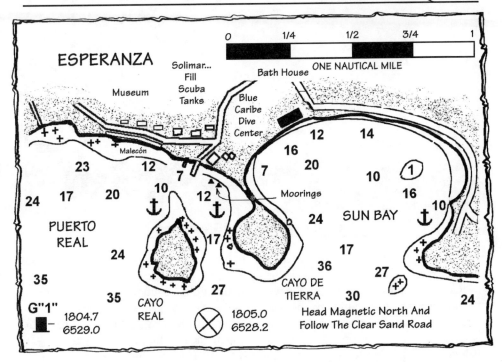

ESPERANZA AND PUERTO REAL

Initially a redoubt of Taino and Caribe Indians from which they could maraud the Spaniards, Vieques became a refuge for all stripes, from army deserters and runaway slaves to the renegade "portugee", as were called the whites of any extraction who were on their own in the Caribbean. Today the island hosts a fiercely independent and p[roud population dotted by (sometimes dotty) expatriates.

SUN BAY

This southern anchorage is outside the Navy zone and next to the fishing village of Esperanza. Enter the middle of the bay headed north, steering clear of the shoal off its southeast arm. Anchor in grassy sand tight against the east southeast shore to avoid roll in strong wind east or south of east. This is a public beach more than a mile in length. A bath house is in the northwest corner of the bay.

Blue Caribe Dive Center maintains moorings at the north end of the anchorage. They are worth the fee to use them, if you wish to use this anchorage. The bottom is Teflon coated grass in fluffy sand. Puerto Real, the anchorage northwest of Cayo Real, can be rolly, but once dug in, the holding is fair in sand and coral. Lunch ashore after a pleasant stroll on the balustraded malecón and a visit to the small archeological museum. For fresh seafood, see the fishermen when they bring in their catches in the morning, or when they gather at the town pier to pack them off on the ferries later on. West of Esperanza, there is a two fathom shoal where seas can build up in strong easterlies or southeasterlies. Official charts notwithstanding, it is marked only by a green can, No. 1, on its eastern edge.

PUNTA ARENAS

A typical weekend at "Green Beach"

Punta Arenas, on the northern end of the western shore of Vieques, is a good stop-over either entering or leaving Vieques Sound. Depending on conditions and wind direction on leaving Palmas del Mar, Punta Arenas may be a better first tack than Isla Palominos. A good anchorage is 40 yards off a flat crescent beach, which the Navy calls Green Beach, and which is one half mile south of Punta Arenas. Another is just south of a ruined dock backed by a couple of large rusty tanks. Head east to the point and turn to the anchorage when in 30 feet of water. Pick a grassy sand spot to avoid the patches of sand colored coral ledges here. The anchorage is isolated on weekdays and the water is clear. Great for bottom scrubbing and skinny dipping. Conch and an occasional lobster are available on the rocky shores to the south. The Escollo de Arenas is the name of extensive sandbores with rock stretching north northwest from the northwest tip of Vieques with only 8-10 feet covering them. Be warned: escollo means trouble. This permanent rocky ridge collects storm detritus for the entire Sound. Though it can be crossed without incident,e ach season some foolish yachtie brags to me that he's gone across the Escollo in a high chop and never saw less than 10 feet. Let

him try it ten times in a row! Donít be fooled by these one time experts. Play it safe. Debris on the bottom can combine with 3 foot troughs to give you a nasty bump on some old wreck or steel tank. I usually go around the Escollo except in a calm. It is a pleasant, reaching sail compared to motor-ing across it.

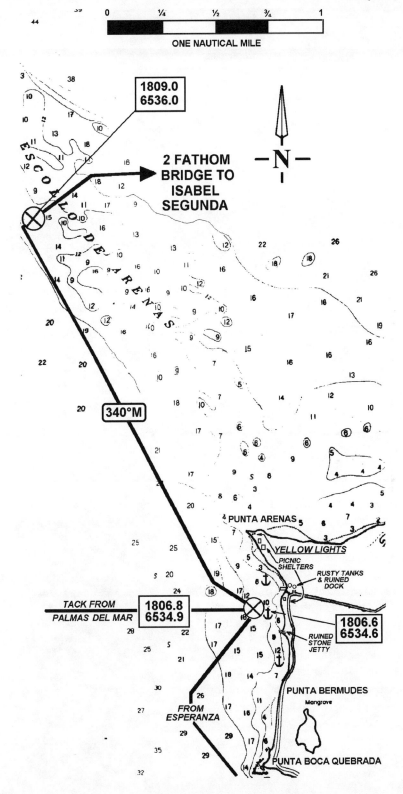

ONE NAUTICAL MILE

1809.0
6536.0

2 FATHOM
BRIDGE TO
ISABEL
SEGUNDA

— N —

ESCOLLO DE ARENAS

340°M

PUNTA ARENAS

YELLOW LIGHTS

PICNIC
SHELTERS

RUSTY TANKS
& RUINED
DOCK

TACK FROM
PALMAS DEL MAR

1806.8
6534.9

1806.6
6534.6

RUINED
STONE
JETTY

FROM
ESPERANZA

PUNTA BERMUDES

Mangrove

PUNTA BOCA QUEBRADA

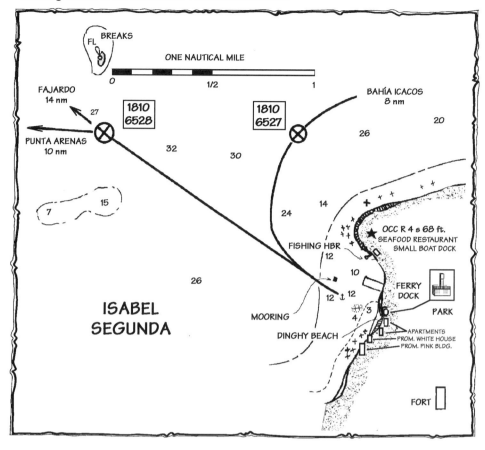

BREAKS

FL

ONE NAUTICAL MILE

0   1/2   1

FAJARDO
14 nm

27

1810
6528

1810
6527

BAHÍA ICACOS
8 nm

20

26

PUNTA ARENAS
10 nm

32

30

7   15

14

24

26

FISHING HBR

12

OCC R 4 s 68 ft.
SEAFOOD RESTAURANT
SMALL BOAT DOCK

ISABEL
SEGUNDA

MOORING

DINGHY BEACH

10

12   12

3

4

FERRY
DOCK

PARK

APARTMENTS
PROM. WHITE HOUSE
PROM. PINK BLDG.

FORT

ISABEL SEGUNDA

Arrive at Isabel Segunda in midmorning in time for a walk up the hill and a visit to the museum and gallery in El Fortín, the Conde de Mirasol fort protecting the harbor. This was the last fort constructed by Spain in the new world. A $20 million resort is in the works on the beach west of here. Visit Isabel Segunda now before the tourist boom.

This anchorage can roll viciously. After a seafood lunch in a harborside restaurant, up anchor in time to make Punta Arenas or Fajardo to the west, or Bahía Icacos to the east, both calm anchorages in prevailing winds and easy to make while the light is still high and westing.

SPANGLISH FOR CRUISERS

The following method to achieve rapid pidgin Spanish, or *Span-glish* as it's sometimes called, is only a guide, not, God forbid, instruction in **Spanish**. The objective here is to permit the totally uninitiated to get things done ashore by employing a pidgin Spanish which can be learned in minutes.

Below is a list of nouns with which the reader joins necessary modifiers and a verb to form a sentence which then can be phonetically read aloud in American English to a listener who will understand it as Spanish. Got that?

Cruisers should worry more about pronunciation than spelling or grammar, since many of the people they talk to ashore can barely read or write anyway. Showing written statements may get you a donation faster than comprehension.

You can successfully talk in nouns only, using your hands for verbs, and pointing around to find descriptors of size, location, color and so on.

All the correct grammar in the world doesn't help the perennial yachtie who goes all over town looking for the hardware store (*ferreteria*) by asking for the furry-TARRY-uh instead of the FAIR-ray-tah-REE-ah. After a few days this type usually goes and sulks on his boat, sails out of the country, and tells stories on the SSB how you can't get anything there and the people are evil.

To accurately name the thing you want you must string together several items from the list of *nouns*. For instance: "motor head bolt". I know it's not called that, but keep it simple. Nothing transliterates.

Talk like an Indian in an old movie: "Ugh! Me need'em motor head bolt". In Latin lingoes you put nouns that modify each other in backward sequence with a *de* [day] between them. A head bolt is bolt of a head. A motor head is a head of a motor. Thus, your movie Indian might say "Ugh! Me need'em bolt of head of motor." So this becomes: "*Oye! Mi necessita tornillo de cabeza de motor*", [me nay-say-SEE-tah tore-KNEE-yo day kah-BAY-tsah day moh-TOR]. Look it up in the following pages.

In this example the pronoun is wrong and the verb is third person, but no matter, you will be clearly understood when quickly reading the phonetics aloud.

Verbs and modifiers are given later for the intermediate student. Those aspiring to black belts can dabble in pronouns and prepositions after that, ensuring massive miscommunication. For now, let's go in search of a bolt for your motor's head. Read on ...

NOUNS

The words given below are often not the most "correct" Spanish but will be useful throughout Latin America because I show common American usage as opposed to European usage. That's no surprise. American English is, after all, significantly different from British English. For example, the word "maní" [mah-KNEE] is used for "peanuts" instead of the Castillano *cacahuete* [kah-kah-WAY-taye]. Both have Indian origins but American Latins never heard *cacahuete* in their lives, and it sounds like something nasty.

Other words, like *suiche* [SWEET-chaye] for "switch", are chosen because, all other parameters being equal, the English speaking boater can remember it easier than other nouns for switches. After all, *suiche* is real Spanglish. It is also the most commonly used form.

Spanish pronunciation or the international semanticist symbology. I chose to mimic the Spanish with written American English as it is commonly spoken.

A speaker of General American will give a good imitation of American Spanish when simply reading aloud the phonetic words below with *strong emphasis* on the capitalized syllables. English words are used when their American pronunciation best simulates the Spanish (e.g., ace and day). Roll your R's if you can but don't sweat it: some Latins don't either.

I spell the American "A" sound "aye", and "I" is spelled "eye". Just read what you see. The Spanish vowels are usually aspirated, that is, using lots of breath. In Spanish, "O" is pronounced "Oh!", "A" is pronounced "Ah!" (as in "father"), "I" is "Eeee...", "E" is "Aye" (as in "say"), "U" is "Oooo...". Thus you will read below *-oh, -ah, -ee, -aye* and *-oo*. Just say them in English.

When listening to Spanish, be careful of "V" and "B". Both sound the same and they are pronounced somewhere between the two. This is true of American Spanish versus the Spanish spoken in Europe. The American hispanics will also drop their "S" sounds. The fewer "S" sounds, the less educated the speaker, normally. It's kind of like "dese" and "dose" in American dialects, but it can really buffalo a foreigner when words whose principal sounds are esses are spoken entirely free of the esses.

Therefore, when the street urchins ask you if you "peek a panich?", they're not asking you to peek at a dirty post card, but they are asking you if you "speak Spanish".

Almost all Spanish speakers add a vowel in front of initial "S" sounds when speaking English because that's what Spanish does. And when the waiter adds an "E" and drops the "S", "spaghetti" can come out "up a Ghetty!" Don't be offended if that's your name.

You'll also notice "Y" is often a "J" sound and double "LL" is a "Y" sound. If you're Judy Yeltsin, they'll spell it Yudy Lleltsin.

Now! Having said all that, here's the list:

acetone	*acetona*	ah-say-TONE-ah
adapter	*adaptador*	ah-DOPT-ah-DOOR
air filter	*filtro de aire*	FEEL-tro day EYE-ray
air vent	*ventil de aire*	vent-EEL day EYE-ray
alternator	*alternador*	all-tern-ah-DOOR
aluminium	*aluminio*	ah-loo-ME-knee-um
amperes	*amperes*	am-PAY-rees
anchor	*ancla*	AN-klah
anchorage	*anclaje*	an-KLAH-hey
avocado	*aguacate*	ah-gwah-KAH-taye
awning	*toldo*	TOLD-oh
back	*posterior*	post-tier-ee-OR
bananas	*guineo*	ee-NAY-oh
band-aid	*curita*	koo-REE-tah
batten	*iston de day vela*	lee-STONE VAYE-lah
battery	*bateria*	bah-taye-REE-ah
beam, boat's	*manga*	MAHN-gah
bearing	*bearing*	BEAR-ring
bilge	*sentina*	sen-TEEN-ah
block	*bloque*	BLOW-kay
block (pulley)	*polea, motón*	poe-LAY-ah, moh-TONE

70

block & tackle	*tecle*	TAYE-clay
boat	*bote*	BOAT-aye
boathook	*botavara*	BOAT-ah-VAH-rah
bollard	*hierro*	E-AIR-roe
bolt	*tornillo*	tore-KNEE-yoh
boom	*botalón*	BOAT-ah-LONE
bottom paint	*pintura de fondo*	peen-TOO-rah day FONE-dough
bow, boat's	*proa*	PRO-ah
brass	*latón*	lah-TONE
bread	*pan*	PAHN
breakwater	*rompeolas*	rome-pay-OH-las
bronze	*bronce*	BRONE-tsay
bulb	*bombilla*	bom-BEE-yah
buoy	*boya*	BOH-jah
bushing	=	BOO-shing
butter	*mantequilla*	mahn-taye-KEY-ya
can	*lata*	LAH-tah
case	*caja*	KAH-hah
catalyst	*activador*	act-tee-vah-DOOR
caulking	*calafate*	cal-ah-FAH-taye
caulking putty	*masilla*	mass-SEE-yah
celery	*apio*	AH-pee-oh
certificate	*certificado*	sair-tee-fee-KAH-dough
chain	*cadena*	kah-DAY-nah
chain plate	*cadenote*	kah-day-NOH-taye
charger	*cargador*	car-gah-DOOR
chart	*carta*	CAR-tah
cheese	*queso*	KAYE-so
circuit	*circuito*	seer-QUEE-toh
clamp	*abrazadera*	ah-bra-sah-DAY-rah
clearance	*despacho*	day-SPAH-cho
cleat	*tojino*	toe-HEE-noh
also....	*cornamusa*	core-nah-MOO-sah
come-along	*gato*	GAH-toh
compass	*brujula*	BRU-hu-lah
conch (DR)	*lambi*	lahm-BEE
conch (PR)	*carrucho*	car-ROO-choo
conch (Ven)	*concha*	CONE-cha
connector	*conector*	coh-neck-TOR
copper	*cobre*	KOH-bray
cotter pin	*passador abierto*	pass-ah-DOOR ah-bee-AIR-toh
coupling	*junta*	HOON-tah
cove	*enseñada*	ain-sane-NAH-dah
crab (DR,Ven)	*congrejo*	cone-GREY-ho
crab (PR)	*jueyes*	HWAY-jace
crew	*tripulante*	tree-pew-LAHN-tay
cushions	*cojines*	co-HEE-nays
customs	*aduana*	ah-DWAH-nah

damage	daño	DAHN-yos
depth	hondura	own-DOOR-ah
diesel	gasoil	gas-OIL
dinghy	lanchita	lan-CHEE-tah
dinghy dock	muellecito	mwaye-yea-SEE-toh
dock	muelle	MWAYE-yea
documentation	documentación	dock-oo-main-tah-see-OWN
dolphin fish	dorado	doh-RAH-dough
draft	calado	kah-LAH-dough
eggs	huevos	WAY-vos
electric	electrico	aye-LAKE-tree-ko
electrician	electricista	aye-lake-tree-SEE-stah
engine	motor	mo-TORE
exhaust	escape	ace-KAH-pay
eye	ojo	OH-ho
eyebolt	tornillo de ojo	tor-KNEE-yo day OH-ho
fathometer	sonda	SOHN-dah
fees	derechos	day-ray-chose
fender	defensa	day-FAIN-sah
fiberglass	fibra de vidrio	FEE-bra day VEE-dree-oh
fins, swim-	chapuletas	chap-oo-LATE-ahs
flag	bandera	bahn-DAY-rah
flashlight	linterna	leen-TAIR-nah
floor	suelo	SWAY-low
fresh water	agua dulce	AH-gwah DOOL-say
front	frente	FRAIN-taye
funnel	embudo	aim-BOO-dough
fuse	fusible	foo-SEE-blaye
garbage	basura	bah-SOO-rah
gas, natural	butano	boo-TAH-no
gasket	junta	HOON-tah
gasoline	gasolina	gas-oh-LEE-nah
gauge	medidor	may-dee-DOOR
generator	generador	hey-nay-rah-DOOR
glue	pegamento	pay-gah-MAIN-toh
grapefruit	toronjas	tore-OWN-hahs
grease	grasa	GRAH-sah
grouper	mero	MAY-roh
guns	armas	ARM-ahs
hammer	matillo	mah-TEE-yo
harbor	puerto	PWAIR-to
harbormaster	capitán de puerto	kah-pee-TAHN day PWAIR-to
hardware store	ferreteria	fair-ray-tah-REE-ah
head (motor)	cabeza	kah-BAY-tsah
head (toilet)	inodoro	een-oh-DOOR-oh
heat	calor	kah-LORE
heat exchanger	enfriadór	ain-free-ah-DOOR
hill	loma	LOH-mah

72

hose	*mangera*	mahn-GAIR-ah
hull	*casco*	kah-skoh
hurricane	*ciclón,*	see-CLONE,
also....	*hurracán*	oor-roo-KAHN
ice	*hielo*	ee-AYE-loh
impeller	*impeledór*	eem-PAY-lay-DOOR
injectors	*inyectores*	een-jake-TORE-ace
insurance	*seguros*	say-GOO-ros
iron	*hierro*	ee-AIR-roh
jack	*gato*	GAH-toh
juice	*jugo*	HOO-goh
kerosene	*kerosena,*	kay-roh-SEE-nah,
also....	*gaz*	GAZ
knot	*nudo*	NOO-dough
l.o.a.	*eslora*	ace-LORE-ah
laundry-place	*lavandaria*	la-VAHN-dah-REE-ah
laundry-clothes	*ropas sucias*	ROPE-ahs SOOj-see-ahs
left	*izquierda*	ees-key-AIR-dah
license	*licensia*	lee-SANE-see-ah
liferaft/vest	*salvavida*	sal-vah-VEE-dah
lighthouse	*faro*	FAH-roh
lights	*luces*	LOOSE-ace
limes	*limónes*	lee-MOAN-ace
line	*linea*	LEE-nay-ah
list	*lista*	LEASE-tah
lockwasher	*arandela de muelle*	ah-rahn-DAY-lah day MWAYE-yea
margarine	*margerina*	mar-hair-EE-nah
marmelade	*mermelada*	MAIR-may-LAH-dah
mask, swim-	*alcafondra*	ahl-kah-FOND-rah
mast	*palo, mastil*	PAH-loh, mah-STEEL
mayonaise	*mayonesa*	my-oh-NAY-sah
meal	*comida*	comb-EE-dah
mechanic	*mecánico*	may-KAHN-ee-Koh
metric	*metrico*	MAY-tree-koh
miles	*millas*	ME-yahs
milk	*leche*	LAYE-chaye
mountain	*montaña*	moan-TAHN-yah
mountain range	*cordillera*	core-dee-YAIR-ah
nail	*clavo*	CLAH-voh
nut (hex)	*tuerca*	TWER-kah
oars (r)	*emos*	RAY-mos
oil	*aceite*	ah-say-EE-taye
oranges	*naranjas*	nar-AHN-hahs
outboard	*fuera borda*	FWAYE-rah BOOR-dah
packing	*empaque*	aim-PAH-kaye
paint	*pintura*	peen-TOO-rah
paintbrush	*brocha*	BROH-chah
parts (spare)	*repuestas*	ray-PWAYE-stahs

peanuts	*maní*	mah-KNEE
pear	*pera*	PAY-rah
pineapple	*piña*	PEE-nyah
pipe	*tubo*	TOO-boh
pistons	*pistones*	pee-STONE-ace
plantains	*plátanos*	PLAH-tah-nos
pliers	*alicates*	ah-lee-KAH-tace
porpoise	*delfín*	dale-FEEN
pressure	*presión*	pray-see-OWN
propane	*propano*	pro-PAH-no
propeller	*hélice*	AYE-lee-say
pump	*bomba*	BOHM-bah
registration	*matriculación*	mah-TREE-koo-Lah-see-OWN
repair	*reparación*	RAYE-pah-RAH-see-OWN
replacement	*repuesta*	raye-PWAYE-stah
resin	*resina*	raye-SEE-nah
regulator	*reguladór*	raye-goo-lah-DOOR
rigging	*járcia*	HAR-see-ah
right	*derecha*	day-RAY-chah
rings	*aníllos*	ah-KNEE-yos
rope	*soga*	SO-gah
rubber	*goma*	GO-mah
rudder	*oja de timón*	OH-ha day tee-MOAN
rust	*óxido*	OAK-see-dough
sail	*vela*	VAYE-lah
sailboat	*velero*	vaye-LAIR-oh
sailcloth	*tela de vela*	TAYE-lah day VAYE-lah
sandpaper	*papél lija*	pah-PAIL LEE-hah
sauce	*salsa*	SAHL-sah
saw	*serrucho*	say-ROO-cho
screw (bolt)	*tornillo maquina*	tore-KNEE-yo MAH-key-nah
screw (wood)	*tornillo madera*	tore-KNEE-yo mah-DAY-rah
screwdriver	*destorneador*	day-STORE-nay- ah-DOOR
scrubbrush	*cepillo*	say-PEE-yo
seacock	llave de toma	YAH-vaye day TOH-mah
seal	*sello*	SAY-yoh
seas	*oleaje*	oh-lay-AH-hey
seasick	*mareado*	mah-ray-AH-dough
seawater	*agua salada*	AH-gwah sah-LAH-dah
shackle	*grillete*	gree-YAYE-taye
shaft	*éje*	AYE-hey
shell	*caracól*	car-ah-COAL
ship	*barco*	BAR-coh
shower	*ducha*	DOO-chah
showers	*aquaceros*	AH-gwah-SAY-ros
shrimp	*camarones*	kah-mah-ROAN-ace
side	*lado*	LAH-dough
smoke	*humo*	OO-moh

snapper	*chillo*	CHEE-yo
soup	*sopa*	SO-pah
sparkplug	*bujía*	boo-HEE-ah
spring	=	ace-SPRING
stainless	*inoxidable*	een-ox-ee-DAH-blaye
stainless (PR)	=	ace-STAIN-less
starboard	*estribor*	ace-tree-BOOR
starter motor	*motór de arranque*	mo-TORE day ah-RAHN-kaye
stay	*soporte de mastíl*	so-PORE-taye day mah-STEEL
steel	*acero*	ah-SAY-roh
stern	*popa*	POPE-ah
storm	*tormenta*	tore-MAIN-tah
straight	*derecho*	day-RAY-choh
strainer	*coladór*	coal-ah-DOOR
street	*calle*	KAH-yaye
stuffing box	*prense*	PRAIN-say
swells	*oleadas*	oh-lay-AH-dahs
switch	*suiche*	SWEET-chaye
tank	*tanque*	TANG-kaye
tape	=	TAYE-pee
tax	*impuesto*	eem-PWAYE-stow
telephone call	*llamada*	yah-MAH-dah
temperature	*temperatura*	taim-pair-ah-TOOR-ah
thermostat	*termostato*	tair-moh-STAH-toh
thinner	*tinner*	TEEN-air
thread (string)	*hilo*	EEL-oh
threads (screw) *roscas*		ROH-skahs
through-hull	*toma*	TOE-mah
tiller	*timón*	tee-MOAN
time	*tiempo*	tee-AIM-poh
tip	*propina*	pro-PEE-nah
tomato	*tomate*	toh-MAH-taye
tools	*herramientas*	air-rah-mee-AIN-tos
top	*parte arriba*	PART-taye ah-REE-bah
transducer	*cebolla*	say-BOY-yah
transmission	*transmisión*	trahns-me-see-OWN
tropical	*tropical*	troh-Pay-KAHL
tropical storm	*tormenta*	tore-MAIN-tah
tropical wave	*onda tropical*	OWN-dah troh-pay-KAHL
turnbuckle	*torniquete*	tore-knee-KAY-taye
two-stroke oil	*aceite dos tiempo*	ah-say-EE-taye dose tee-AIM-poh
valve	*valvula*	VALVE-you-lah
vanilla	=	vahn-EE-yah
varnish	*barníz*	barn-EES
Vee-belt	*banda*	BAHN-dah
vegetables	*vegetales*	vaye-hay-TAHL-ace
volts	*vóltios*	VOLT-ee-os
washer	*arandela*	ah-rahn-DAY-lah

water	*agua*	AH-gwah
watts	*vátios*	VAHT-ee-os
waves	*olas*	OH-las
welding	*soldadura*	sold-ah-DOOR-ah
wheel	*rueda*	roo-AYE-dah
wing nut	*tuerca mariposa*	TWER-kah mar-ee-POSE-ah
wire	*alambre*	ahl-AHM-braye
wood	*madera*	mah-DAY-rah
work	*trabajo*	trah-BAH-ho
wrench	*llave*	YAH-vaye
yacht	*yate*	YAH-taye
zincs	*zinc*	TSINK

VERBS

To talk movie-Indian Spanish, forget the finer distinctions. For instance, use "need" for both "need" and "want". Use "go" for all of the go's, such as come, walk, ride, fly and so forth. The only pronoun you really need is the English "Me", the most important, after all. Everyone else can be identified by pointing a finger.

Just about all of the operable verbs for a *gringo* [GREEN-goh] needing help are below. To use a verb, piece together the words above, in backwards order with lots of *de's* [DAYs] thrown in, and stick a verb on the front. Thus: "BOO-kah tore-KNEE-yo day kah-BAY-tsah day moh-TOR" means, "me look-um for motor head bolt". Don't laugh. It works. If you want to talk better Spanish then learn their 24 (mostly irregular) verb forms. The guy behind the counter is so used to the dumb tricks of *gringos* that he won't blink an eye, but he *will* hand you the bolt. Here are some verbs for the intermediate student:

buy	*compra*	COMB-prah
do, make	*hace*	AH-say
eat	*come*	COMB-aye
find	*consigue*	cone-SEE-gay
go	*va*	VAH
have	*tiene*	tee-AYE-nay
leave	*sale*	SAHL-aye
listen	*oye*	OH-jay
look	*mira*	MEE-rah
look for	*busca*	BOO-skah
need	*necessita*	nay-say-SEE-tah
rent	*renta*	RAIN-tah
repair	*repara*	ray-PAR-ah
sell	*vende*	VAIN-day
sleep	*duerme*	DWAIR-may
talk	*habla*	AH-blah
work	*trabaja*	tra-BAH-hah

You may have noticed the "being" verbs are not included. To use the complex "being" verbs in Spanish can be an art. Better just to not use them. Or just say *es* [ACE], anywhere you want to have "is", "was", "will be" or "might could have been". ACE is great.

NUMBERS

Unlike adjectives, Spanish puts numbers in front of the word they numberfy to make it easy for *gringos*. One *gringo*: *uno gringo*. Two *gringos*: *dos gringos*. And so it goes. Now count to a Zillion *gringos*.

zero	*cero*	SAIR-oh
one	*uno*	OO-noh
two	*dos*	DOSE
three	*tres*	TRACE
four	*cuatro*	QUAH-troh
five	*cinco*	SINK-oh
six	*se's*	SAY-ees
seven	*siete*	see-AYE-taye
eight	*ocho*	OH-cho
nine	*nueve*	NWAYE-vaye
ten	*diéz*	dee-ACE
eleven	*once*	OWN-say
twelve	*doce*	DOSE-say
thirteen	*trece*	TRAY-say
fourteen	*catorce*	kah-TORE-say
fifteen	*quince*	KEEN-say
sixteen	*diéz y se's*	dee-ACE ee SAY-ees
seventeen	*diéz y siete*	dee-ACE ee see-AYE-taye
eighteen	*diéz y ocho*	dee-ACE ee OH-cho
nineteen	*diéz y nueve*	dee-ACE ee NWAYE-vaye
twenty	*veinte*	VAIN-taye
twenty-one	*veinte uno*	VAIN-taye OO-noh etc.
thirty	*treinta*	TRAIN-tah fourty
forty	*cuarenta*	quar-AIN-tah
fifty	*cincuenta*	seen-QUAINT-ah
sixty	*sesenta*	say-SANE-tah
seventy	*setenta*	say-TAIN-tah
eighty	*ochenta*	oh-CHAIN-tah
ninety	*noventa*	no-VAIN-tah
one hundred	*ciento*	see-AIN-toh
two hundred	*dos cientos*	DOSE see-AIN-tos
thousand	*mil*	MEAL
million	*millón*	me-YONE

For example, 1989: *mil novecientos ochenta nueve.*

You can now say you're looking for <u>two</u> motor headbolts: BOO-kah DOSE tore-KNEE-yo day kah-BAY-tsah day moh-TOR" — and you don't have to go shopping twice to get them!

MODIFIERS

If you must modify a noun, do so by putting the modifiers in backwards order but without all the *de* [DAY] stuff you put between the nouns when you strung them together. Thus "two big black motor head bolts" is "two bolts of head of motor black big", or,

> BOO-kah DOSE tore-KNEE-yo day kah-BAY-tsah day moh-TOR GRAHN-day NAYE-grow.

And just like in English, let everyone guess if it's the motor or the bolts which is big and black or is it a combination of both.

COLORS

black	*negro*	NAYE-grow
blue	*azúl*	ah-TSOOL
brown	*marrón*	mar-ROAN
green	*verde*	VAIR-day
grey	*gris*	GREASE
orange	*naranja*	nah-RAHN-hah
pink	*rosado*	rosa-AH-dough
red	*rojo*	ROH-hoh
white	*blanco*	BLANK-oh
yellow	*amarillo*	ah-mah-REE-yo

ADJECTIVES AND ADVERBS

big	*grande*	GRAHN-day
broken	*roto*	ROH-toh
cheap (thing)	*barato*	bah-RAH-toh
clean	*limpio*	LEEM-pee-oh
closed	*cerrado*	say-RAH-dough
cold	*frio*	FREE-oh
deep	*hondo*	OWN-dough
different	*diferente*	dee-faye-RAIN-taye
dirty	*sucio*	SOO-see-oh
down	*abajo*	ah-BAH-ho
dry	*seco*	SAY-koh
electrical	*electrico*	aye-LAKE-tree-ko
expensive	*caro*	CAR-roh
fast	*rapido*	RAH-pee-dough
fine	*fino*	FEE-noh
fixed-repaired	*reparado*	ray-pah-RAH-dough
fixed-unmoving	*fijado*	fee-HAH-dough
galvanized	*galvanizado*	gal-van-ee-SAH-dough
heated	*calientado*	kah-lee-ain-TAH-dough
heavy	*pesado*	pay-SAH-dough
high	*alto*	AHL-toh
hot	*caliente*	kah-lee-AIN-taye
less	*menos*	MAY-nose

light	*ligero*	lee-HAIR-oh
little	*no mucho*	NO MOO-cho
long	*largo*	LAHR-go
loose	*flojo*	FLOW-ho
low	*bajo*	BAH-ho
more	*mas*	MAS
open	*abierto*	ah-bee-AIR-toh
portside	*babor*	bah-BOOR
same	*mismo*	MEESE-moh
self-tapping	*autorroscante*	ow-toe-ros-KAHN-taye
shallow	*bajita*	bah-HEE-tah
slow	*despacio*	day-SPAH-see-oh
small	*pequeño*	pay-CAIN-yo
thick	*grueso*	grew-ACE-oh
thin	*delgado*	dell-GAH-dough
tight	*apretado*	ah-pray-TAH-dough
up	*arriba*	ah-REE-bah
wet	*mojado*	moh-HAH-dough
wide	*hancho*	AHN-cho

PAST AND FUTURE

Movie Indians conjugate their verbs by modifying them with a word like "yesterday". Thus "Me need'um head bolt yesterday. Today need'um band-aid". So, say anything you want in present tense and add from the following list:

today	*hoy*	OY
tomorrow	*mañana*	mah-NYAH-nah
yesterday	*ayer*	ah-JAIR
last night	*anoche*	ah-NO-chaye
day before yesterday	*ante* ayer	auntie ah-JAIR
...days ago	*hace.....dias*	AH-say.....DEE-ahs
...weeks ago	" *...semanas*	" ...say-MAH-nahs
...months ago	" *...meses*	" ...MACE-ace
...years ago	" *...años*	" ...AHN-yos
next week	*proxima semana*	PROHKS-ee-mah say-MAH-nah
next month	*proximo mes*	PROHKS-ee-moh MACE
next year	*proximo año*	PROHKS-ee-moh AHN-yo

PREPOSITIONS

These are the condiments the advanced students will sprinkle onto their crude sentences in order to throw the hearer off the track. Proper use requires years of practice.

after	*después* de	days-PWACE day
before	*antes* de	AHNT-ace day
between	*entre*	AIN-tray
by	*por*	PORE
to	*á*	AH

for	*para*	PAH-rah
from	*de*	DAY
in	*en*	AIN
inside	*dentro de*	DAIN-troh day
of	*de*	DAY
on	*en*	AIN
under	*abajo de*	ah-BAH-ho day
with	*con*	CONE
without	*sin*	SEEN

PRONOUNS

Finally, for the black belters, peppering a fancy construction with pronouns will ensure confusion but impress the dickens out of fellow yachties. These are the advanced student's tools with which to make clear that which was better off left vague. When instead of a big, black head bolt for your motor, the guy behind the counter hands you two tickets to the cock fights, if you are a real black belt student you say, *grácias*, and thread your way through the throng of thunderstruck fellow boaters with a satisfied grin and just the hint of a swagger. You can get the headbolts tomorrow; today go to the cockfights.

Once again, this short list of pronouns is only to enable you to rapidly employ a pidgin Spanish which works, not to speak properly.

Now you're able to say "ME look'um for 2 big black motor head bolts FROM THEM TOMORROW". Or,

ME BOO-kah DOSE tore-KNEE-yo day kah-BAY-tsah day moh-TOR GRAHN-day NAYE-grow DAY AYE-yos mah-NYAH-nah.

I	*yo*	JOE
you	*tu*	TOO
he	*él*	AYEL
she	*ella*	AYE-ya
it	*lo*	LOW
we	*nosotros*	no-SO-tros
you all	*ustedes*	oo-STAID-ace
they, them	*ellos*	AYE-yos
this	*esto*	ACE-tos
that	*eso*	ACE-oh
each	*cada*	KAH-dah
which	*cual*	QUAL
something	*algo*	AHL-go
nothing	*nada*	NAH-dah
other,another	*otro*	OH-troh
any, -thing, -body	*cualquier*	qual-key-AIR
all, everybody -thing, -one	*todo*	TOE-dough
none,nobody, no one	*ninguno*	neen-GOO-noh
some, -body, -one	*alguién*	ahl-kee-AIN

QUESTIONS

Questions are best asked as statements with lots of body language, helpless expressions and the voice turned up in pitch toward the end, even panicky, as in

DOAN-day me BOAT-aye?!

for "Where's my boat?!" A very important question if it's gone.

You can also make up a declarative sentence as shown above and slap any one of the following words on the front to have a neat question to go to town with:

how	*como*	KO-moh
how much	*much cuanto*	QUAN-toh
when	*cuando*	QUAN-dough
where	*donde*	DOAN-day
who	*quién*	key-AIN
why	*porqué*	pore-KAY

But beware of asking why or how. You may get a torrent of rapid Spanish. Also, beware to phrase your questions bluntly in movie-indian talk. For instance, "I wonder if you could tell me where I might find oil pressure transducers for sale?" becomes "Where sell oil pressure transducers?" or:

DOAN-day VAIN-day say-BOY-yah day pray-see-OWN day ah-say-EE-taye?

— accompanied by a lot of shrugs and wiggling of the eyebrows. Other questions are:

What is it?	Que es eso?	KAY ACE ACE-oh
What's it/he/she called?	Como se llama?	KO-moh say YAH-mah?
What time is it?	Que hora es?	KAY OR-ah ACE?
At what time?	A que hora?	AH KAY OR-ah?
How far?	Que lejos?	KAY LAY-hos?
Where is it/he/she?	A donde está?	AH DOAN-day ace-TAH?
What's it cost?	Cuanto cuesta?	QUAN-toh KWAYE-stah?
How do I get there?	Como llegaré?	KO-moh yaye-gar-RAY?
Can you help me?	Puede ayudarme?	PWAY-day ah-you-DAHR-may?
How do you say...?	Como se dice..?	KO-moh say DEE-say...?
What do you mean?	Que quiere decir?	KAY key-AIR-aye day-SEER?
What does it mean?	"	"

Index

H

Haiti   39
hauling out   25
high tide 27
hose   23
Humacao   25
hurricane   29
hydraulic hose   23

I

Icacos   5
insurance   16
Isabel Segunda   68
Isla Chiva   63
Isla Palominos   49
Isla Yallis   62
Isleta   25
Isleta Marina   46

L

language barriers   12
Las Croabas   25
Las Hermanas   53
Laying Anchor   19
Lexan   23
log   27
logs   27
Los Galafatos   63
Los Gemelos   53
Luis Peña   49, 52, 53

M

Mail   11
Manzanillo   39
Master Charge   23
Mayaguana   39
Monte Pirata   61

N

nylon rode   21

P

Palmas del Mar   25, 49
Palominos   5
Pasaje Medio Mundo   43

Piedra Steven   53
Pilot Charts   26
piracy   14
Pirates   14
Ponce   23
Ponce Yacht Club   23, 25
Provisioning   23
Públicos in Puerto Rico   3
Puerto del Rey   45
Puerto Ferro   64
Puerto Mosquito   64
Puerto Plata   39
Puerto Real   25, 45, 46
Punta Arenas   49, 68
Punta del Noroeste   53
Punta Lima   42

R

radio direction finder   30
RAFA   23
Reed's Nautical Almanac   26
Repairs   23
Roosevelt Roads   49

S

Salinas   23
Salinas de Sur   61
scope   21
seals   23
Security 14, 16
security   17
sextant   28
Spanish Virgins   47, 49
SSB   30
SSBs   31
Stainless   23
stainless 23
Sun Bay 64, 65

T

Teflon   23
Telephone   11
theft   16, 17
tide   26
Tide Tables   26
tropical waves   5